AFRICA: PROGRESS & PROBLEMS

LIBERTY
THE LOVE OF
BROUGHT US
REPUBLIC OF LIBERIA
THE
CONSTITUTION
OF THE

AFRICA: PROGRESS & PROBLEMS

THE MAKING OF MODERN AFRICA

Tunde Obadina

Mason Crest Publishers
Philadelphia

Frontispiece: In January 2006 Ellen Johnson-Sirleaf is sworn in as Liberia's first female president, becoming Africa's first elected woman head of state. Some people consider the increase in multiparty democratic elections and peaceful transitions of power in African nations as indicators of positive growth in the continent.

Produced by OTTN Publishing, Stockton, New Jersey

Mason Crest Publishers
370 Reed Road
Broomall, PA 19008
www.masoncrest.com

Printed and bound in India.

First printing

1 3 5 7 9 8 6 4 2

Library of Congress Cataloging-in-Publication Data

Obadina, Tunde.
The making of modern Africa / Tunde Obadina.
p. cm. — (Africa : progress and problems)
Includes bibliographical references and index.
Audience: Grades 9-12.
ISBN-13: 978-1-59084-998-9
ISBN-10: 1-59084-998-1
1. Africa—History—Juvenile literature. 2. Africa—Colonial influence—Juvenile literature. 3. Africa—Social conditions—Juvenile literature. 4. Africa—Economic conditions—Juvenile literature. I. Title.
DT22.023 2007
960—dc22

2006022238

TABLE OF CONTENTS

AFRICA: PROGRESS & PROBLEMS

AIDS AND HEALTH ISSUES

CIVIL WARS IN AFRICA

ECOLOGICAL ISSUES

EDUCATION IN AFRICA

ETHNIC GROUPS IN AFRICA

GOVERNANCE AND LEADERSHIP IN AFRICA

HELPING AFRICA HELP ITSELF: A GLOBAL EFFORT

HUMAN RIGHTS IN AFRICA

ISLAM IN AFRICA

THE MAKING OF MODERN AFRICA

POPULATION AND OVERCROWDING

POVERTY AND ECONOMIC ISSUES

RELIGIONS OF AFRICA

THE PROMISE OF TODAY'S AFRICA

by Robert I. Rotberg

Today's Africa is a mosaic of effective democracy and desperate despotism, immense wealth and abysmal poverty, conscious modernity and mired traditionalism, bitter conflict and vast arenas of peace, and enormous promise and abiding failure. Generalizations are more difficult to apply to Africa or Africans than elsewhere. The continent, especially the sub-Saharan two-thirds of its immense landmass, presents enormous physical, political, and human variety. From snow-capped peaks to intricate patches of remaining jungle, from desolate deserts to the greatest rivers, and from the highest coastal sand dunes anywhere to teeming urban conglomerations, Africa must be appreciated from myriad perspectives. Likewise, its peoples come in every shape and size, govern themselves in several complicated manners, worship a host of indigenous and imported gods, and speak thousands of original and five or six derivative common languages. To know Africa is to know nuance and complexity.

There are 53 nation-states that belong to the African Union, 48 of which are situated within the sub-Saharan mainland or on its offshore islands. No other continent has so many countries, political divisions, or members of the General Assembly of the United Nations. No other continent encompasses so many

distinctively different peoples or spans such geographical disparity. On no other continent have so many innocent civilians lost their lives in intractable civil wars—12 million since 1991 in such places as Algeria, Angola, the Congo, Côte d'Ivoire, Liberia, Sierra Leone, and the Sudan. No other continent has so many disparate natural resources (from cadmium, cobalt, and copper to petroleum and zinc) and so little to show for their frenzied exploitation. No other continent has proportionally so many people subsisting (or trying to) on less than $1 a day. But then no other continent has been so beset by HIV/AIDS (30 percent of all adults in southern Africa), by tuberculosis, by malaria (prevalent almost everywhere), and by less well-known scourges such as schistosomiasis (liver fluke), several kinds of filariasis, river blindness, trachoma, and trypanosomiasis (sleeping sickness).

Africa is the most Christian continent. It has more Muslims than the Middle East. Apostolic and Pentecostal churches are immensely powerful. So are Sufi brotherhoods. Yet traditional African religions are still influential. So is a belief in spirits and witches (even among Christians and Muslims), in faith healing and in alternative medicine. Polygamy remains popular. So does the practice of female circumcision and other long-standing cultural preferences. Africa cannot be well understood without appreciating how village life still permeates the great cities and how urban pursuits engulf villages. Half if not more of its peoples live in towns and cities; no longer can Africa be considered predominantly rural, agricultural, or wild.

Political leaders must cater to both worlds, old and new. They and their followers must join the globalized, Internet-penetrated world even as they remain rooted appropriately in past modes of behavior, obedient to dictates of family, lineage, tribe, and ethnicity. This duality often results in democracy or at

least partially participatory democracy. Equally often it develops into autocracy. Botswana and Mauritius have enduring democratic governments. In Benin, Ghana, Kenya, Lesotho, Malawi, Mali, Mozambique, Namibia, Nigeria, Senegal, South Africa, Tanzania, and Zambia fully democratic pursuits are relatively recent and not yet sustainably implanted. Algeria, Cameroon, Chad, the Central African Republic, Egypt, the Sudan, and Tunisia are authoritarian entities run by strongmen. Zimbabweans and Equatorial Guineans suffer from even more venal rule. Swazis and Moroccans are subject to the real whims of monarchs. Within even this vast sweep of political practice there are still more distinctions. The partial democracies represent a spectrum. So does the manner in which authority is wielded by kings, by generals, and by long-entrenched civilian autocrats.

The democratic countries are by and large better developed and more rapidly growing economically than those ruled by strongmen. In Africa there is an association between the pursuit of good governance and beneficial economic performance. Likewise, the natural resource wealth curse that has afflicted mineral-rich countries such as the Congo and Nigeria has had the opposite effect in well-governed places like Botswana. Nation-states open to global trade have done better than those with closed economies. So have those countries with prudent managements, sensible fiscal arrangements, and modest deficits. Overall, however, the bulk of African countries have suffered in terms of reduced economic growth from the sheer fact of being tropical, beset by disease in an enervating climate

where there is an average of one trained physician to every 13,000 persons. Many lose growth prospects, too, because of the absence of navigable rivers, the paucity of ocean and river ports, barely maintained roads, and few and narrow railroads. Moreover, 15 of Africa's countries are landlocked, without comfortable access to relatively inexpensive waterborne transport. Hence, imports and exports for much of Africa are more expensive than elsewhere as they move over formidable distances. Africa is the most underdeveloped continent because of geographical and health constraints that have not yet been overcome, because of ill-considered policies, because of the sheer number of separate nation-states (a colonial legacy), and because of poor governance.

Africa's promise is immense, and far more exciting than its achievements have been since a wave of nationalism and independence in the 1960s liberated nearly every section of the continent. Thus, the next several decades of the 21st century are ones of promise for Africa. The challenges are clear: to alleviate grinding poverty and deliver greater real economic goods to larger proportions of people in each country, and across all 53 countries; to deliver more of the benefits of good governance to more of Africa's peoples; to end the destructive killing fields that run rampant across so much of Africa; to improve educational training and health services; and to roll back the scourges of HIV/AIDS, tuberculosis, and malaria. Every challenge represents an opportunity with concerted and bountiful Western assistance to transform the lives of Africa's vulnerable and resourceful future generations.

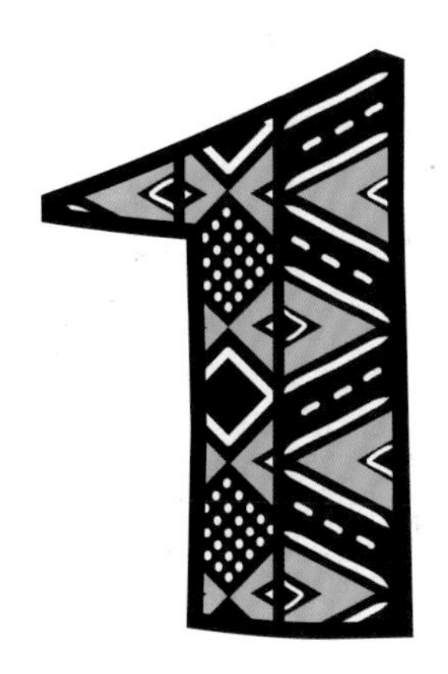

DEFINING AFRICA

The identity of the African people as Africans comes in part from a shared history of dealing with foreign imperialism and slavery.

The continent of Africa can be described in many different ways. In geographical terms, it is the world's second-largest continent, stretching from the northernmost point of Tunisia to the southernmost tip of South Africa. Bordered to the west by the Atlantic Ocean and to the east by the Indian Ocean, the continent contains environments varying from arid deserts, to semi-arid savannas, to dense rain forests.

Africa can also be described as the oldest inhabited territory on earth. Approximately 4 million years ago the continent provided the setting for the evolution of the human race. At that time ape-like creatures named *Australopithecus afarensis* walked upright on two feet in the continent. Another 2 million years later a new species, *Homo erectus*, appeared in Africa. These first humans walked long distances in search of food and developed a technology based on sharp tools made of flint, during an era later known as the Stone Age. About a million years ago these early humans began to leave Africa and migrate to other continents, beginning the process in which humans populated the planet.

Africa is also defined by its present-day inhabitants. The continent does not have one people, one history. Its population of more than 900 million features a variety of different peoples, who speak an assortment of more than 1,000 languages and represent cultures just as vast and varied. In Africa's most populous nation, Nigeria, more than 250 ethnic groups speak over 400 different languages.

THE AFRICAN PEOPLE

Africa is sometimes described as comprising two distinct regions, defined largely in terms of the racial origin of their respective inhabitants. There is North Africa, made up of Arabic-speaking nations (Algeria, Libya, Egypt, Morocco, and Tunisia), which is home to approximately 200 million people. The rest of the continent, commonly referred to as sub-Saharan Africa, is occupied by a population of more than 700 million, which is predominantly black.

However, Africans from all parts of the continent commonly dispute such regional division. They argue that defining themselves as either Arab northerners or black southerners is not only based on faulty geographic, political, and cultural considerations but also ignores the diversity found in both regions and the links between them. Some North Africans resent being identified as belonging to Arab nations simply because of their lighter complexion.

For many people living outside the continent, the term *Africa* is more than a geographical expression. It implies that the people living on the continent share a common identity based on certain shared attributes, such as history, economic experience, culture, and self-identity. When journalists report that Africa is in crisis or that more should be done to end Africa's poverty, this suggests that Africans or their nations share common conditions beyond occupying a distinct geographical land mass.

PAN-AFRICANISM

Today, many people living in the continent view themselves as Africans, and not as northerners or southerners, or as members of one of the continent's 53 nations. A useful definition of *nation* is a collection of people who have come to believe that they have been shaped by a common past and are destined to share a common future. Nationalism is a commitment to fostering these beliefs and promoting policies to achieve the ideals of the nation.

This concept of nationalism has been extended in Africa to encompass the whole continent. Called pan-Africanism, this belief emphasizes the concept of a united African nation. The idea of Africa as a single political and cultural entity has evolved within the context of the interaction between the diverse peoples of the continent with those from outside the region. In fact, forces from outside the continent, particularly Western European imperialism, have shaped much of Africa's history.

EUROPEAN IMPERIALISM AND COLONIALISM

Imperialism refers to the practice of one country imposing its control, directly or indirectly, over the territory, political system, or economic life of another country. Critics of imperialism say that its prime purpose is the transfer of wealth from the acquired territory to the imperial center through the exploitation of its people and resources.

Some African historians say that the first stage of Western European imperialism occurred with the establishment of the large-scale transatlantic slave trade, which began during the

1500s. According to this perspective on history, African societies shared the common experience of being made part of Europe's trading empires.

The second stage involved colonialism, when European countries extended their sovereignty over African territories and people. Through this wave of European imperialism, which occurred between the late 19th century and early 20th century, African societies suffered economically, politically, and culturally.

AFRICAN NATIONALISM

The development of pan-Africanism and African nationalism emerged largely as a response to European domination of the

Africa's political, economic, and cultural development was disrupted by the practice of slavery. It drained the continent of its people, as millions were sent into forced labor in the Americas. During the brutal passage overseas, several hundred captives would be crammed into a small slave ship, with little access to food or water.

continent. Although the ancient Romans apparently first referred to the region as Africa, it was not until the 19th century that the term *Africa* and its derivative *African* came into common usage among the peoples living in the continent. Before European colonization, the inhabitants of Africa saw themselves as belonging to communities. They had no reason to conceive of themselves as members of a larger community beyond their local boundaries. However, by the late 19th century, many community leaders, or elites, had come to view Africa as supranational—that is, transcending national boundaries.

These educated elites saw that Africa had particular social, economic, and political problems that needed to be addressed as an entire continent. This perspective of pan-Africanism led to various political movements, in which nationalists both in the homeland and in the African diaspora sought to unite African communities, end colonialism in Africa, and achieve self-governance.

IMPACT OF GLOBALIZATION

Africa's history has been greatly influenced by globalization—the movement of people, goods, services, and capital throughout the world. One of these influences in the making of modern Africa was the transatlantic slave trade. Another was European colonialism, which fundamentally altered boundaries of nations in the continent.

European imperialism also helped bring about the emergence of a common identity among the African people, who shared the experience of colonialism. Subsequently, the identity of modern Africa can be said to have developed out of the cultural dislocation resulting from globalization.

EARLY HISTORY

Not much is known about Africa's earliest history, although many scholars believe that early people originated around the Rift Valley of eastern Africa more than 3 million years ago. Over the next several thousands of years, these early humans gradually moved north and established numerous settlements along the Nile River, in northeastern Africa.

One of the most powerful and long-lasting of these early civilizations was Egypt, which some scholars believe began around 3400 B.C. The Nile River sustained the agriculture economy of the Egyptian civilization and allowed it to develop in a region with unreliable rainfall and poor soil.

Other early African civilizations, such as the Kushite and Meroitic, were also sustained by the Nile. The Nile Valley region, flanked by desert to the west and equatorial jungle to the south, evolved at first in isolation from the rest of Africa.

EARLY NILE VALLEY CIVILIZATIONS

Ancient Egypt is one the earliest known civilizations in the world, famous for its development of hieroglyphic writing and its achievements in agriculture, art, and architecture. The splendor of its civilization is still evident today in its ancient pyramids and its tombs, which have been uncovered by archeological digs. Ruled by leaders known as pharaohs, Egypt reached its height around 1570–1342 B.C. However, the country's fortunes declined during the first millennium B.C., when it was invaded and conquered by a series of foreign powers.

By then the Egyptian culture had spread further south along the Nile, to Nubia, located in today's southern Egypt and northern Sudan. The Nubians, who were black Africans,

One of the best-known early African civilizations, Egypt produced architectural wonders that still stand today. This photo shows 19th-century Nubian soldiers at the Step Pyramid, located in Saqqara, near modern-day Cairo. Built around 2600 B.C., the structure was Egypt's first pyramid and, at 204 feet (62 meters) high, the largest building of its time.

developed the Kingdom of Kush in the Sudanese Nile Valley from 2000 B.C. onwards. Egypt conquered Kush, which was a valuable trading center, in 1500 B.C., but was in turn conquered in 750 B.C. by the Kushites, who founded the 25th dynasty of pharaohs.

The Kushite state was quite prosperous, with its capital first at Napata and then further south along the Nile, at Meroe (near modern-day Khartoum, Sudan). Around 1400 B.C., with the development of iron-making technology, Meroe became an important center for ironworking.

By the 4th century A.D. Meroe had declined, perhaps overthrown by the kingdom of Aksum (also known as Axum), a major state in today's northern Ethiopia. Aksum dominated the Red Sea both commercially and militarily from the first century A.D. until around the 7th century.

WEST AFRICA: THE KINGDOM OF NOK

As the practice of farming spread to the west into West Africa, many settlements sprang up along the Niger River, in modern-day Nigeria. During the first millennium B.C., some of these civilizations also developed ironworking technology. The first iron-smelting civilization in West Africa was the Nok, whose people also established widespread livestock and cereal agricultural societies.

The Nok civilization of West Africa lasted from around the 5th century B.C. to the 2nd century A.D. In addition to making iron weapons and tools for farming, Nok metalworkers made jewelry and small iron figures used in rituals to mark births, marriages, and deaths. The culture also was renowned for its pottery: Nok artisans created realistic terracotta sculptures of heads and figures.

The arts of iron technology and agriculture spread to other parts of sub-Saharan Africa, carried by Bantu-speaking peoples who were influenced by the Nok culture. Descendants of these early agriculturalists who moved south from Nigeria occupy almost all of sub-equatorial Africa today.

Artisans of the Nok civilization, which developed in West Africa between the Niger and Benve Rivers around 500 B.C., created fired clay sculptures such as this one. Although the Nok culture ended around 200 A.D., its elaborately stylized terracotta artwork continued to influence future African civilizations.

NORTHWESTERN AFRICA: GHANA AND MALI

Around 750 A.D., as the camel became a common means of transporting goods, trade routes developed through the Sahara Desert between cities in the Maghreb (the region north of the desert) and cities in sub-Saharan Africa. The first kingdom to establish full control over the southern end of the Saharan trade route was Ghana. The Ghana Empire, which eventually encompassed present-day Mali, southern Senegal, and southern Mauritania, sat at the crossroads of trade routes leading north, south, east, and west. By the early 9th century Arab traders were spreading word of the wealthy empire, describing it as "the land of gold," because of its exclusive control on trade in the precious metal.

Other products that passed through the empire included cloth and luxury items from Europe, as well as ivory, leather goods, and kola nuts from countries in the south. Also traded were slaves bought and taken by Arab traders across the Sahara to be resold as servants in the Mediterranean and Near East. The most common goods that went south from Ghana were salt (found in large quantities in the desert and essential to the diet of African agricultural communities), dates, and a wide range of metal goods, including weapons. By the end of the 12th century, the Ghana Empire had declined as it lost its trading monopoly and its major gold mines became less productive.

A new empire that derived much of its wealth from goldfields in Bure, near the Upper Niger Valley in modern-day Guinea, soon arose. It was led by Sundiata Keita, ruler of a small Malinke kingdom that had been part of the Ghana Empire. In 1240 he established the Mali Empire, with its first capital, Niani, on the Upper Niger River. Sundiata Keita eventually created a vast empire that at its largest reached about 1,250 miles (around 2,000 km) wide. It stretched from the Atlantic coast south of the Senegal River to the kingdom of Gao (on the Niger River) and northeast to Tadmekka (in the southern Sahara).

The people of Mali benefited from their proximity to the Niger River. Mali farmers developed the fertile land surrounding the Niger, and exported their produce to the north by boat. Merchants also used the waterway to trade gold, kola nuts, and slaves in exchange for cloth, copper, dates, figs, metal goods, and salt. With its monopoly on the gold and salt trades, the Mali Empire prospered for many years.

During the 14th century the empire reached its peak. At that time its leader, Mansa Musa, established Timbuktu as the capital. Scholars and merchants from other parts of Africa, the Middle East, and even Europe came to Timbuktu, renowned as a center of learning and trade and for its universities and bustling markets. Mansa Musa also used Mali's wealth to build stunning buildings in other Mali cities, including Gao, Jenne, and Niani. Following his death, however, the Mali empire began to decline. By 1500 Mali had been eclipsed by the burgeoning Songhay kingdom in the east, which established Gao as its capital.

THE HAUSA STATES AND THE BORNU EMPIRE

East of Mali, just south of the Sahara Desert, lay another strong African empire. The Hausa people had first established communities there in 900 A.D. By the late 12th century, these small communities had joined together, forming the seven city-states of Kano, Zaria, Gobir, Katsina, Rano, Daura, and Biram. Because their people shared a common language (Hausa), the city-states commonly traded among themselves. Some, particularly Zaria, Kano and Katsina (all located in present-day Nigeria), became very prosperous.

Berber nomads known as Tuaregs barter in the 1950s walled marketplace of Timbuktu, a former capital of the Mali Empire. Established in 1100 A.D., the city served merchants traveling the salt caravan trade routes that crossed through the Sahara Desert.

During the 15th century, the Hausa states became closely allied with the Kanem–Bornu Empire (in modern day Chad). Northeast of Lake Chad, the Kanem Empire had been founded in the 9th century A.D. by a confederation of Saharan tribes. The Hausa kingdoms and cities in the Kanem–Bornu Empire prospered as important terminals along the trade routes that served the Berber people of North Africa and forest people of the south.

YORUBALAND AND BENIN

Other organized states existed south of the Sahara Desert, in the tropical forest regions of Africa, but these kingdoms tended to be small and isolated. Unlike the open ṣavannah of the north, where small communities could easily coalesce into larger and more powerful states, the tropical rain forests in the south presented barriers to the unification of villages and towns. Still, some forest states became prosperous and powerful. Among them was the Yoruba kingdom of Ife.

Example of Yoruba sculptures. The Yoruba kingdoms included the cities of Ife and Oyo, which were located in modern-day southwest Nigeria and Benin. Yoruba artisans were renowned for figurines and sculptures created of terracotta, brass, and wood.

Founded by the Yoruba people around 500 B.C., Ife had grown into a major artistic center by 900 A.D. Located west of the Niger River and south of Hausaland, the city reached its peak between the 13th and 15th centuries, when it was regarded as the most powerful of the Yoruba kingdoms. Ife is famous for its ancient bronze, stone, and terracotta sculptures, which some scholars say were influenced by the art of the Nok culture. Early Ife art demonstrates levels of craftsmanship comparable with the finest examples of Renaissance metal-work in Europe.

During the 15th century another Yoruba kingdom, called Oyo, surpassed Ife in political and economic power. Founded around the 1400s in the savanna north of the forest, Oyo benefited from its strategic location along trade routes between the north and south. Its cavalry forces came to dominate its surrounding regions during the 17th and 18th centuries. Eventually the Oyo Empire encompassed several other Yoruba states as it stretched eastward toward the present-day Republic of Benin, just south of Ife.

Located in modern-day Nigeria, the Benin Empire was another powerful civilization that reached its height during the 15th century. Founded around the 10th century A.D., with Benin City as its capital, the prosperous empire was famous for its wealth and its art, especially the bronze and ivory sculptures of the heads of its rulers and their wives.

The Benin Empire was first visited by Europeans in the mid-1480s. At that time Portuguese explorer Joao Afonso Aveiro described the capital as the "great city of Benin." Over a hundred years later, around 1600, a Dutch visitor noted that the African city was much like the European city of Amsterdam:

> As you enter [Benin], the town appears very great. You go into a great broad street, not paved, which seems to be seven or eight times broader than the Warmoes Street in Amsterdam. . . . The houses in this town stand in good order, one close and even with the other, as the houses in Holland stand.

MAPUNGUBWE EMPIRE

Large African empires also developed in lands much farther to the south. During the 13th and 14th centuries one of the largest kingdoms in Africa's subcontinent was Mapungubwe. Located at the extreme northern border of modern-day South Africa, at the confluence of the Limpopo and Shashe Rivers, the kingdom thrived as an important trading center in southern Africa. Most of its wealth came from cattle production and the mining of gold.

Ruins and tower of Great Zimbabwe, a stone-fortified city built in southern Africa by the Shona people of the Mapungubwe Empire in the late 11th century. Its 32-foot-high curved walls, built without mortar, amazed German explorer Carl Mauch, the first European to encounter the ruins in 1871. He and many others refused to believe that black Africans had built the city, and instead credited its existence to an unknown race.

Inhabited by the Shona people, the Mapungubwe kingdom was first established in 900 A.D. It eventually covered an area that encompassed parts of the modern states of Zimbabwe and Mozambique. The empire flourished as the center of an international commercial trading network that included numerous settlements along the East African coast, as well as China, Persia, Egypt, and India.

Toward the end of the 1300s drought conditions in Mapungubwe forced its inhabitants to migrate further north, where many settled in the city of Great Zimbabwe. Founded in the late 11th century, the city featured massive stone buildings and high, curved walls. During the 15th century Great Zimbabwe became a center of Shona power, housing at its peak as many as

30,000 people. In addition to its reputation as a major trading center, Great Zimbabwe was well known for the fine pottery and sculpture of its artisans, as well as for the sophisticated stonework of its structures. Scholars theorize that famine or the changes in gold trade operations led the people of Great Zimbabwe to abandon the city around 1500.

KONGO

Another major African state emerged during the early 15th century in the region south of the lower Congo River, along the west coast of Africa. The Kongo kingdom evolved from a loose federation of several communities ruled by a monarch called the Manikongo. The kingdom was rich in resources, including fertile soil for farming and iron and copper ore deposits for mining. The Congo River allowed the people to establish an extensive trading network that reached thousands of miles. Among the crafts produced and traded by the people of Kongo were metalwork, pottery, copperware, and raffia textiles (made from the fibers of the raffia palm tree).

At its peak Kongo was the biggest state in western central Africa. Bordered by the Atlantic Ocean to the west, Kongo included parts of present-day northern Angola, the Republic of the Congo, and the Democratic Republic of the Congo.

THE SWAHILI

Along the eastern coast of Africa a number of settlements arose that—although connected by language—did not exist as an empire, but as separate city-states. They were inhabited by people who spoke primarily Bantu, with elements of Arabic. The resulting combined language is known as Swahili. By the 1300s, coastal Swahili city-states could be found as far north as Mogadishu (in modern-day Somalia) and as far south as Sofala (in today's Mozambique). Other major city-states included

Mombasa (in Kenya) and Kilwa (on the island of Zanzibar, in Tanzania).

These Swahili cities evolved over the course of years of trade that began around the 2nd century A.D. between the people of the East African coast and merchants and traders from Arabia, Persia, India, and China. From around 900 A.D. onward, some of these traders, especially Arabs from the Persian Gulf, settled along the east coast of Africa. As they established colonies and trading towns and married local African women, the Swahili ethnic group evolved, with its own distinct architecture, culture, and music.

The east coast of Africa had a long history of trade. Chief exports included ivory, rhino horn, sandalwood, tortoise shell, textiles, and gold. However, interaction among cultures also involved the exchange of ideas as well as goods. As the Arab presence on the east coast of Africa increased, the Islamic religion took root. By the 1300s, the Swahili city-states had become major Islamic cultural centers.

CHRISTIANITY AND ISLAM

The religions of Christianity and Islam both came to Africa from outside the continent. Christianity, based on the teachings of Jesus Christ, arrived in Africa first, brought by missionaries to Egypt sometime during the first or second century A.D. By the 4th century the religion had spread along the trade routes from Egypt to northeastern Ethiopia, where the king of the Aksum Empire converted. He established the Ethiopian Orthodox Church, one of the first Christian churches in the world. However, while Christian orthodoxy reached into parts of Sudan and other neighboring regions, it did not spread to the rest of the continent. Instead, another faith took hold.

The Islamic faith is based on the teachings of the prophet Muhammad, who lived from 571 A.D. to 632 A.D. The religion was first introduced into North Africa in 639 A.D., when the

Holding the holy book of Islam, the Qur'an, a Swahili man reads before fellow Muslims in the city of Lamu, Kenya. The Islamic faith spread rapidly in Africa after its introduction into the continent during the 7th century A.D. By the 14th century the religious faith was firmly established in East Africa, where the Swahli people lived.

army of the Muslim Arab General Amir ibn al-Asi invaded Egypt. His army, inspired by the new religion, began a conquest of Africa that moved westward.

Islam establishes detailed instructions on how people are expected to behave in both private and public spheres. Because the religious faith requires adherence to specific rules in areas such as governance and administration, Islamic communities shared a culture that was distinct from that of traditional African societies.

Africans chose to convert to Islam for several reasons. It offered previously fragmented and antagonistic groups of people common bonds of government and broader fellowship. The faith was tolerant of most African customs, and often incorporated traditional African values, although in moderation. For example, the indigenous custom of polygamy (having more than one wife) was allowed, as Islamic law permits men to have up to four wives.

By 705 A.D. the Maghreb had become an integral part of the Islamic world. Islam also spread southward along the East African coast, carried by merchants plying the well-established trade routes. By the 8th century the religion had reached as far south as Kenya. By the 11th century, when Islam made its biggest advances in Africa, several Muslim communities had been established down the east coast of the continent.

Arab traders who crossed the Sahara to the west during the 8th century and in the years that followed also carried their religious faith with them. Over the centuries, they converted many West Africans to Islam. By the 11th century some West African rulers had converted to the faith. During the 14th century, the West African empire of Mali, led by Mansa Musa, had become an important Islamic hub and the city of Timbuktu a center of Muslim scholarship. Islam also spread peacefully throughout sub-Saharan Africa, usually through Arab traders.

Islam and Christianity replaced traditional African faiths, which typically were based on a belief in one supreme god, although some peoples such as the Yoruba also believed in the existence of many less powerful deities. According to African traditional teachings and customs, everyday life was influenced by the spirits present within nature and of one's departed ancestors. Worshipers believed that prayer and sacrifice allowed one to communicate with the spiritual world. Some traditional African customs included fetishism (belief that an object has magical powers that can help its owner) and the worship of animals.

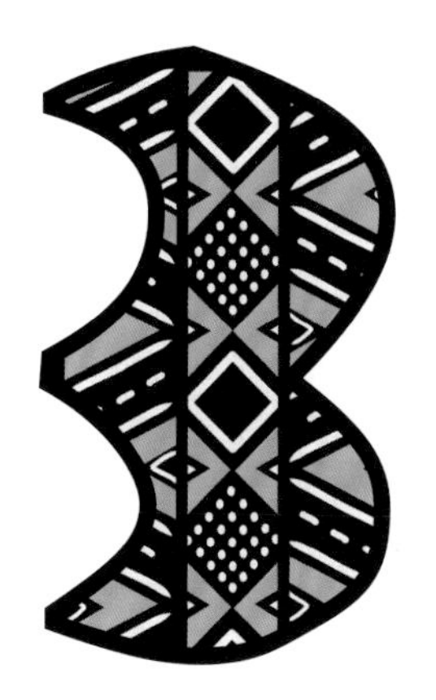

EUROPEAN INCURSION

While vast and powerful empires in Africa rose and fell over the centuries, up until the middle of the 15th century few people in Europe knew these kingdoms even existed. Eventually Arab merchants and traders who had visited the continent began to spread word about inland empires in Africa with great wealth. Such tales inspired 15th century European sea traders to search for a land south of the Sahara Desert, called Guinea, which was said to be filled with gold.

PORTUGUESE EXPLORATION

The first European explorers to Africa came from Portugal. A dominant trading force in Europe during the 15th century, Portugal sought an alternative to the overland route through the Sahara Desert. When they landed on the Guinea Coast in the 1440s, Portuguese seamen became the first Europeans to reach sub-Saharan Africa by sea. By 1513 the Portuguese had established trading posts along Africa's east coast, and in many coastal ports replaced the Arabs in the gold trade.

In addition to gold, the Portuguese also trafficked in slaves. From the outset Portuguese sailors seized Africans and shipped them to Europe. In 1441 ten kidnapped Africans were taken to Portugal as gifts to its ruler, Prince Henry the Navigator. In subsequent expeditions to the West African coast, more inhabitants were captured and taken to Portugal to be sold to wealthy households as servants and as objects of curiosity.

THE SLAVE TRADE

Although trafficking in Africans by Europeans was not a major commercial activity in the beginning, it quickly became a highly profitable enterprise as European nations established colonies in the New World (as the continents of North and South America were known). Colonial settlement in the Caribbean and South America by the Spanish marked the beginning of a triangular trade network in which European slave ships took people from Africa to the Caribbean and the Americas and brought back New World products to Europe. In 1518, the year that King Charles I of Spain authorized the slave trade from Africa to the New World, the first shipment of African-born slaves arrived in the West Indies.

As early as 1482 the Portuguese established numerous trading posts along the shoreline of the Gold Coast (in today's Ghana), where they built castles that served as holding stations for slaves being sent overseas. Portugal maintained a monopoly on the slave trade in Africa until the 16th century, when England, followed by France and other European nations, entered the profitable business. The rapidly growing demand for sugar and tobacco that began during the 17th century fueled the demand for slave labor, resulting in a significant increase in the triangular slave trade.

The business of the slave trade was lucrative for foreign merchants, who exchanged European goods for captured Africans. This 1729 engraving of an English slave trader and African suppliers of slaves at Fort de Maures on the island of Moyella, West Africa, illustrates how slave transactions were documented on paper, giving them legal standing.

Between 1500 and 1900, millions of Africans were captured and shipped out of the continent. Estimates of the total number of Africans affected vary widely. Conservative estimates contained in Angus Maddison's *The World Economy: Historical Statistics* put the number of black African slaves exported to the Americas during this time at just over 11 million. Other historians estimate the number to be 15 million or more. During the same period another 3.2 million black Africans were taken across the Sahara to serve as slaves in Europe and almost 2 million more were kidnapped and sent to Asia.

The first European-built structure south of the Sahara Desert was Elmina Castle, located on the southern cape coast of modern-day Ghana. Constructed by the Portuguese in the 15th century, the castle was used as a holding station for slaves destined for the New World.

The actual number of African lives lost as a result of the slave trade was far greater than the amount sold into slavery. The real casualty toll includes the many people who perished in slave-generating wars and conflicts, as well as those who died during the long, brutal passage to their final destination.

AFRICANS ENSLAVING AFRICANS

During the initial stages of the slave trade, Europeans captured Africans in raids on communities in the coastal areas around Africa. Such tactics later gave way to the general practice of Europeans buying slaves from African rulers and merchants—although the Portuguese remained directly involved in capturing slaves further south in Angola.

Many African rulers, traders, and military leaders grew wealthy from the slave trade business, and were in fact responsible for selling the majority of the slaves taken out of the continent. Large numbers of slaves were obtained through wars that were sometimes fought primarily to capture people for enslavement. It had long been the custom of warring African states with hierarchical structures to make their prisoners slaves, but the commercial profits from the rapidly growing Atlantic slave trade gave an added impetus to go to war.

After a visit to Benin in the early 1500s, Portuguese explorer Duarte Pacheco Pereira wrote that the kingdom "is usually at war with its neighbors and takes many captives, whom we buy at twelve or fifteen brass bracelets each, or for copper bracelets, which they prize more." A large number of people were kidnapped while going about their everyday tasks or captured during slave raids on poorly protected communities. Some African rulers who did not engage directly in the capture and transportation of slaves nevertheless profited by collecting taxes on slave-related transactions in their domain.

At the time the transatlantic slave trade took place, there was little understanding of the concept of universal human rights, including the right to life and liberty. Ideas of human freedom and individuality were at best underdeveloped in all parts of the world. In Africa, people lived in societies in which their loyalty lay with their extended family and community, so the idea of capturing and enslaving members of another community, especially one that was a rival for limited resources (such as land or water), may not have seemed immoral.

In addition, other forms of slavery or near slavery existed in other parts of the world. During the 17th and 18th centuries large numbers of poor whites were shipped to the New World, most involuntarily, to work on plantations, mines, and in households as servants. Some poor whites kidnapped on European streets were sold in the West Indies much in the same way as Africans were. Indentured white servants, convicts, and deportees from Europe were often treated not much better than black slaves, working hard under extremely harsh conditions and with short life expectancy. Like slaves, the indentured servant was regarded as a piece of property and was valued according to the amount of sugar and tobacco that he or she could be expected to produce before the indenture expired.

Plantation owners in the New World initially looked to the indigenous Indian population for labor, then to white convicts or indentured labor, and then to black slaves. The transatlantic slave trade boomed after it became clear that other sources of cheap labor could not meet the growing demand. It was the relative low cost of African slaves, and therefore the plantation owners' preference for them, that led to the ending of trade in white labor and increased demand for Africans.

Not all African rulers who had the opportunity to participate in the transatlantic slave trade did so. The Jola people of Casamance (in modern-day Guinea and Senegal) refused to negotiate with European slave traders and forbade the passage of captives through their domain. In Ghana, King Tanja Musa built two walls around Gwolu City to prevent slave raiders and slave traders from entering. Although the king of Benin had initially allowed slave trafficking in his domain, after 1530 he banned the sale of slaves. He, like many other rulers in Africa, had come to realize that the trade was harmful to the kingdom, because it drained the community of laborers and wealth.

IMPACT ON AFRICA

The slave trade devastated African societies in many ways. It undermined the potential that African societies may have had for industrialization by establishing the region as only a supplier of labor. The few manufacturing activities that existed in Africa were either destroyed or denied conditions for growth. As cheap European textiles and iron and steel goods were imported into Africa as payment for slaves and primary commodities, local production of similar products was undermined.

In addition, the numerous wars waged to procure slaves not only destroyed human lives, but also bred hostility and distrust within and among African communities. As a result, Africa's small communities did not unite and form large states that could have fended off foreign incursions.

Many historians have argued that the slave trade also undermined Africans psychologically and arrested the cultural development of their societies. The dehumanizing commercial slave trade affected the meaning that people gave to the world and their place within it. Because of their uncertainty of life and liberty, Africans commonly sought salvation and protection through superstitious beliefs, such as paying homage to gods to safeguard themselves and their families from misfortune.

By the time the slave trade reached its peak in the late 18th century, the kidnapping and delivery of slaves to European trading posts in the coastal areas of Africa was firmly under the control of Africans. At that time one of the richest markets for slave traders was the Gold Coast. In many parts of continent, the slave trade had become so integral to the economy that African rulers and merchants resisted efforts by the British to suppress it after Great Britain outlawed the trade in 1807 and banned slave ownership in 1834.

The dependence of some of Africa's ruling classes on slave trafficking was so great, English missionary and abolitionist Thomas Buxton wrote in 1840, that the best way to suppress the trade was to offer Africa's slaving elites an alternative, legitimate business. Then they would have the means to satisfy their hunger for European goods. "The African has acquired a taste for the civilized world," Buxton wrote. "They have become essential to him. To say that the African, under present circumstances, shall not deal in man, is to say he shall long in vain for his accustomed gratification."

During the rest of the 1880s numerous countries outlawed slavery. However, the transatlantic slave trade did not come to an end until slavery was abolished in Brazil in 1888.

END TO THE SLAVE TRADE

The main factors that led to the end of slavery were events that took place outside Africa. During the latter half of the 18th century, the Industrial Revolution in Britain and the emergence of modern capitalism brought about fundamental changes in the nature of economic production and trade.

The Industrial Revolution refers to the technological changes that took place during the 18th century that resulted in work

After Great Britain outlawed the international slave trade in 1807, British warships began patrolling the west coast of Africa in an effort to end the practice. The British navy would seize ships suspected of engaging in the trade, but slavery continued in some African nations well into the late 1800s. This 19th century image shows a group of African men and boys in the hold of a British warship, after being rescued from slavers.

being done by machines rather than by manual labor. Capitalism refers to an economic system based on the voluntary exchange of goods and services between private individuals and business firms operating in a free market (one in which prices of goods are free from government interference and regulation). Capitalism is based on the use of free labor, not slave labor. As explained by the 18th century economist Adam Smith in his book *The Wealth of Nations*, slave labor is less productive than free labor, especially in the manufacturing sector. Enterprises using slaves tend to be less innovative and dependent on physical labor, while those employing freemen are more innovative and inclined to invest in machinery. As Western economies became more industrialized, the demand for slave labor decreased.

At the same time, attitudes toward slavery were changing, in part because of an early 18th century intellectual movement in Europe that extolled the ideals of human progress, liberty, property, and rationality. Later referred to as the Age of Enlightenment, because its supporters advocated ideas of universal liberty and equality to peoples in both Europe and the Americas, the movement is said to have encouraged black leaders like General Toussaint L'Ouverture of Saint-Domingue (now Haiti) who in 1791 helped instigate a successful slave uprising.

Out of this enlightened humanitarianism grew secular and religious antislavery movements in Britain, France, and the United States. However, in Africa itself the concepts of individual liberty and opposition to the absolute power of monarchs did not yet take root.

COLONIAL RULE

(Opposite) During the second half of the 19th century the Swahili trader and slave merchant Tippu Tib (reclining) helped several Arab sultans establish large domains in east and central Africa. He also negotiated with European representatives such as the British diplomat Leander Starr Jameson (seated in chair), who helped Great Britain obtain mineral concessions in Matabeleland and Mashonaland (present-day Zimbabwe).

During the first 80 years of the 19th century, European powers did not look to acquire and rule over territories in Africa. In fact, as of 1875 Europeans controlled less than 10 percent of the continent. However, by the end of the 1800s European nations had embarked on a policy of imperial colonial expansion. Their ensuing race to acquire and control African land became known as the "Scramble for Africa."

Conflicts among European countries, notably Portugal and France, over territorial claims to land around the mouth of the Congo River led to a meeting of all European powers with colonial interests in Africa in Berlin, Germany. At the Berlin Conference of 1884–85, European governments established rules and boundaries for the division of the continent among themselves.

By 1914 most of the African continent had been colonized. Only Ethiopia (which successfully resisted occupation) and Liberia (which had been founded by the American Colonization Society) were not under colonial rule.

MOTIVATION FOR COLONIZATION

The factors that spurred European interest in the colonization of Africa are many. There was the desire to secure supplies of raw materials for fast-growing European industries and to capture markets for their products. This quest for markets and sources of raw materials is evident in the comment made by American explorer Henry Morton Stanley a few years before the formal colonization of Africa. At a meeting of businessmen in 1872, Stanley described the potential for trade within the continent:

> There are forty millions of people beyond the gateway of the Congo and the cotton-spinners of Manchester [England] are waiting to clothe them. Birmingham [England] foundries are glowing with red metal that will presently be made into ironwork for them and the trinkets that shall adorn those dusky bosoms.

Some historians have argued that European powers did not need to subjugate underdeveloped countries to attain their

economic objectives. These scholars contend that most societies in Africa and elsewhere in the world would have freely traded with the industrializing nations without first being colonized.

However, advocates of colonialism presented expansion as a "civilizing" mission that Europeans embarked upon for both practical and altruistic reasons. They insisted that European rule was necessary to establish the infrastructure and institutions, such as the rule of law and a modern judicial system, that were required for underdeveloped societies to be integrated into a global capitalist market.

Another contributing factor to the drive for colonies was ongoing competition among industrialized nations. During the 1800s Britain's economic position in the world was declining, as countries such as the United States and Germany were gaining power. To maintain economic strength, the British needed to find new markets for their goods. Further motivating European nations to control African land was the desire to defend their established trading posts in Africa from encroachment by rival countries.

Industrializing European nations could facilitate overseas expansion through technological developments produced by the Industrial Revolution. For example, advanced systems of transportation (steam navigation, railroads) and communications (the telegraph) made it easier for European governments to dispatch personnel to colonies and administer territories. At the same time medical advances, especially the discovery of quinine as treatment for the deadly disease of malaria, enabled Europeans to safely penetrate the interior of Africa.

The Industrial Revolution was also accompanied by the growth of a free market economy, in which individuals rather than governments set prices of goods. The free market philosophy calls for the elimination of any social and political constraints that may hinder business transactions. During the late 19th century and early 20th century, the idea of free trade was dominant in the countries of Europe and the United States. Many industrialists and politicians believed it was in the mutual interest of people in developed (industrial) and underdeveloped societies to link their economies.

DIVIDING UP AFRICA

The partition of Africa among European nations fundamentally changed the face of the continent. France acquired the biggest amount of land, colonizing Algeria, Tunisia, and Morocco in North Africa. France also took over eight countries in West Africa, and four in central Africa, as well as Somaliland (Djibouti), Madagascar, and Comoros in the east.

However, Great Britain took the largest population and probably the most strategically important areas of the continent. The British controlled Egypt in the north; Sudan, Kenya, and Uganda in the east; Sierra Leone, The Gambia, Nigeria, and the Gold Coast (collectively referred to as British West Africa); and most of southern Africa.

In 1882 British interests in North Africa had resulted in the invasion and occupation of Egypt, as part of the United Kingdom's effort to secure the 100 mile-long Suez Canal. The French-built canal across the Isthmus of the Suez provided a vital shipping lane between the Mediterranean Sea and the Red Sea. A major factor in Britain's decision to expand colonial control was the desire to protect the sea routes to India, a British colony since the 1850s. Through the Berlin Conference, the British took control of lands stretching from Egypt to South Africa.

Although the Portuguese had been the first Europeans to set up trading posts in Africa, at the time of the Berlin Conference Portugal had become a relatively weak European power. It obtained only Angola (in southwest Africa) and Mozambique (in southeast Africa), as well as a few small territories in West Africa.

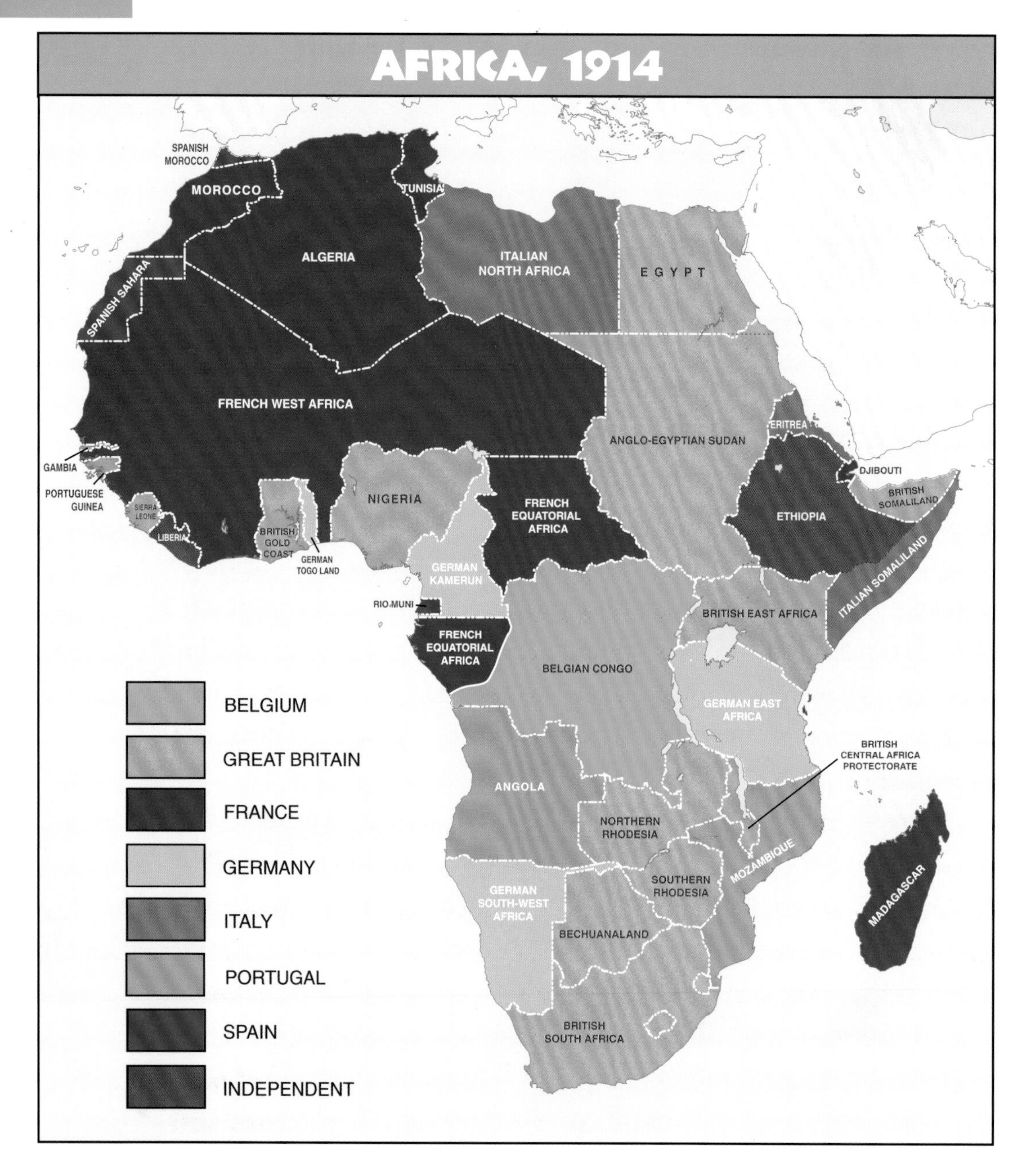

By 1914 the "Scramble for Africa" had ended with the major European powers laying claim to most of the continent. At that time Great Britain and France held control over the greatest amounts of land.

Germany took Togo and Cameroon (in West Africa), Namibia (southwest Africa), and German East Africa (which would later become Tanganyika, Burundi, and Rwanda). However, following its defeat in the First World War

(1914–1918), Germany lost these colonies to other European nations.

Other portions of the continent were divided among smaller European powers. Spain colonized the Western Sahara and a few other minor territories. Belgium possessed the Congo, a vast territory at the center of Africa.

The boundaries drawn by the imperial powers were artificial and sometimes illogical. Many cut across existing cultural lines and divided ethnic nations that had held together for centuries. For example, the Masai people of East Africa were split between German-ruled Tanganyika and British-ruled Kenya. Yoruba communities in West Africa were divided between French-ruled Benin and British-ruled Nigeria. In French-speaking Senegal, the British made claim to a narrow strip of land that encompassed the Gambia River. The newly formed country, named The Gambia, divided the Mandinka and Wolof peoples of Senegal into two colonies administered by two European powers that spoke different languages.

RESISTANCE TO EUROPEAN RULE

As European powers penetrated Africa, their armies often managed to establish control over territories without having to use much force. Authority over regions was generally obtained through treaties and agreements reached with local rulers.

The superiority of the military forces of the colonizing powers to those of most African armies contributed to the ease with which colonial powers conquered some small states. While the firepower of the Africans and Europeans had been comparable in the early 1800s, European governments possessed far superior firepower by the latter half of the century. Faced with Maxim machine-guns (the world's first automatic machine gun, capable of firing approximately 500 rounds per minute), Africans carrying single-shot rifles or bow and arrows stood little chance.

The European armies that went into Africa were small in number, but well equipped. Once they established control over local governments, they commonly filled their ranks with members from the indigenous population.

Several factors contributed to the acceptance of colonial rule in many parts of Africa. At the time, the people in communities suffering from activities of the slave trade welcomed the intervention of European powers as a means to stop human trafficking and impose order. Political and military elites who might have organized resistance to European incursion often wanted to participate in the material-rich economy that the colonialists promised. In some African societies, the people welcomed colonial rule because it created new avenues for social and economic mobility outside the traditional, rigid hierarchical order. The colonial system, with its government bureaucracy and foreign commerce, enabled new classes to emerge. Africans who joined the colonial government or engaged in modern business received monetary benefits from the new order, and subsequently had an interest in defending it.

In areas where communities had been engaged in long-term wars or hostilities linked to slave trading, the ability to form military alliances against the European imperialists had been severely weakened. Some communities actually invited the colonialists to help them fight their neighbors. Under such conditions it was easy for the European powers to apply divide-and-rule strategies to gain and maintain dominance.

However, some states in Africa put up a fight against European encroachment. In 1896 the Abyssinians (in modern-day Ethiopia), under Emperor Menelik II, defeated the Italians at the Battle of Adowa. Well over 100,000 Sudanese died fighting superiorly armed British forces (who suffered fewer than 50 killed) as they conquered the Mahdist government in 1898 during the Battle of Omdurman. There was also resistance in many places where large numbers of Europeans took over African lands or imposed unfair taxes on local communities.

At the 1896 Battle of Adowa, Emperor Menelik II successfully repelled the Italian attempt to acquire his Ethiopian kingdom during the First Italo-Abyssinian War. Unlike its neighbors, which fell under colonial rule, Ethiopia remained an independent nation.

CONTRASTING STYLES OF COLONIAL RULE

The form of colonial governments established in Africa varied according to the European power in control. The French approach to colonial rule was highly centralized and made little effort to involve local rulers. France pursued a policy of assimilation, in which colonial subjects were converted to the French culture.

In contrast, the British established an indirect style of government, ruling where possible though the local monarchs or chiefs. Britain did not have an official policy of acculturation. Its colonial administrators did little to reform the feudal system they found in Africa. Indeed, in some places they saw themselves as defenders of the traditional African ways, and thus endeavored to keep away any outside cultural influences.

Colonial rule evolved differently in regions such as eastern and southern Africa, where large white settler populations were established. The large influx of European settlers often led to conflicts between the indigenous people and the newcomers.

EUROPEAN SETTLEMENT IN SOUTHERN AFRICA

One of the regions that attracted early European settlement was southern Africa, in the Cape of Good Hope, where the Dutch East India Company established an outpost in 1652. The company brought Dutch settlers who farmed and raised stock on land that later became known as the Cape Colony.

Gradually the Dutch colony expanded north and east, displacing the region's indigenous peoples, the Khoikhoi and the San. In resulting hostilities, the Dutch and their descendants, who came to be called Afrikaners, took the land and cattle of local people and sometimes enslaved them. Many Khoikhoi became slaves to the Dutch in 1659 after losing a battle over grazing land rights.

Tensions between the two groups intensified with the presence of ever-increasing numbers of European settlers in South Africa. Between the late 18th century and mid-19th century, numerous frontier wars erupted between the Europeans and another South African indigenous group, the Xhosa people, mainly over land and cattle. By 1854 the British had stripped the Xhosa chiefs of power and incorporated them into the colonial administration.

At the end the 18th century, Great Britain seized the Cape Colony from the Dutch, and it became a British colony. European migration from Cape Colony increased dramatically around 1835, when many Afrikaners, looking to escape British rule, moved to lands to the east and northeast in what became known as the Great Trek. The Afrikaners (also known in their language, Afrikaans, as Boers, meaning "farmers") founded republics such as the Transvaal and the Orange Free State, which they considered outside British control. However, between 1899 and 1902 the British won the Transvaal, and by

1910 had absorbed the Afrikaner republics, thereby creating the Union of South Africa.

The mineral wealth of southern Africa fueled European territorial ambitions, particularly after the discovery of diamonds in the late 1860s and gold in the 1880s. As a result, more Europeans immigrated to the region. Among them was the English adventurer and diamond magnate Cecil Rhodes, who led the initiative to exploit the region's mineral resources. His vision of imperial rule in Africa saw Britain controlling the continent from the Cape to Cairo, Egypt.

In 1888 King Lobengula of the Matabele signed an agreement with the British South Africa Company in which he relinquished mineral rights to his land. Later, in an attempt to keep growing numbers of white settlers out of his kingdom, Lobengula took up arms against the British. He was defeated in 1893, and died the following year.

Among the lands that Rhodes acquired for Britain was the Ndebele kingdom, in today's Zimbabwe. In 1888 King Lobengula was tricked into signing a document giving away the mineral rights to the land. Rhodes subsequently used the document to persuade the British government to grant his company, the British South Africa Company (BSAC), a royal charter. When Lobengula objected to the mining of gold and to colonist encroachment on Ndebele land, the British military invaded and defeated the African king's army. The British and their Boer allies subsequently took control of the land and confiscated the cattle.

In 1896 the African people of the region rose in revolt, but their uprising was brutally suppressed. Many African prisoners of war were hanged en masse. Eventually the contested territory was named Rhodesia, in honor of Cecil Rhodes, and ruled by the BSAC under its royal charter. Large numbers of whites flocked to Rhodesia from South Africa and were allocated land taken from Africans.

EUROPEAN SETTLEMENT IN NORTH AFRICA

Extensive European settlement also occurred in parts of North Africa such as Algeria. France had first invaded Algeria in the 1830s, but it took several decades before the French could establish complete control of the country and its longtime inhabitants, the Berbers. Subsequently, Europeans from France, Italy, and Spain began to occupy the land, taking over farmland and valuable properties that had been confiscated from African owners. By the end of the 19th century, Algerians of European descent were considered French citizens, while Muslim Algerians refused to accept French citizenship.

COLONIAL OPPRESSION AND RACISM

Colonial rule was particularly oppressive and dehumanizing for Africans in the Belgium colony, which had been established in the Congo during the Berlin Conference. Belgium King Leopold II treated the territory as his personal fiefdom, giving much of the land to concessionaire companies, some of whom used slave labor to collect rubber. The king, facing huge debts at home, used a regime of terror to compel Africans to collect rubber. If people did not collect enough rubber, they were killed and their severed hands sent back as proof of their death. After reports of these and other atrocities were publicized, Leopold was compelled by the Belgium parliament in 1908 to hand over the territory to the Belgium government, which took over administration of the colony.

The Germans were also harsh colonial masters. In German South-West Africa (now Namibia) the German government attempted to exterminate the Herero and Nama peoples after they revolted in 1904 over the payment of taxes and seizure of their lands. The Germans pursued a military campaign of genocide, driving the two ethnic groups into the Kalahari Desert without food or water. These actions resulted in the deaths of some 55,000 Herero (about 80 percent of the total population) and 10,000 Nama (about half the total population).

From 1885 to 1908 King Leopold II of Belgium ruled over the Congo Free State, subjecting its inhabitants to a reign of exploitation and terror. If the African villagers living in the colony did not meet the required quota of wild rubber, they were severely punished—with beatings, by having hands cut off, or with death.

Because of the relatively large presence of whites in settler colonies, the manifestations of racism were greater there than in places with fewer European settlers, although native populations suffered humiliation in those regions as well. In South Africa, the Afrikaners' belief in white racial superiority led to the development of the apartheid system in that country. Apartheid, which comes from the Afrikaans word for "apartness," refers to the policy of segregation and discrimination against non-European groups that took place in South Africa. White-minority governments in Rhodesia and Kenya also institutionalized racial segregation.

RELIGION

The greatest foreign cultural influence on African societies came through the religious conversion, to Islam or Christianity, of people throughout the continent. Over time the traditional faiths of a majority of Africans were replaced by one of these two faiths. Although Christianity was introduced into Africa earlier, by the end of the 19th century Islam had secured a stronger hold. In the 1880s approximately one third of the continent was Muslim.

However, during the late 19th century, as European colonialism became widespread on the continent, Protestant and Catholic workers poured into Africa, many from missionary movements established to convert the "heathens" of the world. Christian missionaries not only built churches but also opened schools and hospitals, working tirelessly to convert people to their faith.

Large numbers of people living in western and southern Africa, as well as in parts of East Africa, enthusiastically adopted Christianity, and their conversion had profound consequences on African societies. Because reading the Bible is essential in Christianity, missionary schools helped previously illiterate Africans learn to read, in either English or an African language. However, the Christian doctrines the missionaries taught derided many traditional African customs and beliefs as barbaric and uncivilized. Missionaries criticized the practice of polygamy and required converted Africans to be monogamous. Christian leaders condemned fetishism and demanded an end to the worship of animals. Missionaries criticized the wearing of African clothes and promoted Western European attire. The imposition of Western European culture on African society changed the ways that the indigenous people viewed themselves, and altered their understanding of the world and their place within it.

INFLUENCE OF WESTERN CULTURE

Western cultural influences also came to Africa from African ex-slaves who returned to the continent after living in other countries. Most of these former slaves settled in Freetown, in Sierra Leone, and in Monrovia, in Liberia.

In 1787 British abolitionists sent freed slaves from England to a settlement along the west coast of Africa, in today's Sierra Leone. A few years later they were joined by a number of ex-slaves from Nova Scotia, Canada, who officially founded the city of Freetown in 1792. The town's population continued to grow with the arrival in 1800 of the Maroons—slaves who had rebelled against the British in Jamaica and originally been deported to Canada.

In 1808 Freetown became a British crown colony, and its inhabitants soon built up thriving communities. Within a few decades of landing, many former penniless slaves and their descendants had acquired affluent lifestyles much like those of their middle-class contemporaries in Europe and the Americas.

With European colonization came Christian missionaries, who converted hundreds of thousands of Africans to the Protestant and Roman Catholic faiths. Christianity promoted literacy and education in Africa, but also denigrated many aspects of its traditional culture.

These freed slaves and their descendents, called Creoles, made up the majority of the professional, intellectual, and merchant classes of 19th century West Africa.

To the south of Sierra Leone, freed slaves from the United States established Liberia in 1822. The colony became an independent republic in 1847, with Monrovia as its capital. The descendents of American slaves, referred to as Americo-Liberians, controlled the country's politics, although they made up a minority of the population and were greatly resented by the indigenous people. As in Sierra Leone, the former slaves and their descendants produced educated elites of professionals—in areas such as medicine, law, administration—and took less to trade and business.

Freed slaves and their descendants in both Sierra Leone and Liberia formed elite groups that were European in culture. Some became missionaries, helping to spread the creed of Christianity. Others became influential intellectuals who challenged

Founded in 1792 by former slaves from Nova Scotia, Canada, the African city of Freetown was subsequently settled by thousands of freed slaves from the United States and Jamaica. The city served as the capital of British West Africa from 1808 to 1874.

European theories of racism and ethnocentrism (the belief that one's own group or culture is superior to all other groups or cultures). Few African elites supported traditional African customs and beliefs. In fact, most were as contemptuous of African culture as whites were.

RACIAL IDEOLOGY

The colonization of Africa was accompanied by racism—the belief that a person's race determines his or her capabilities and that certain races are inherently superior or inferior to others. Numerous pseudoscientific writings on race appeared in Europe during the later half of the 19th century. The majority of these publications asserted that the white race was superior to all other races. White explorers, academics, slave traders, and plantation owners commonly portrayed Africans as inferior and barbaric, either inherently incapable of improvement or capable only when under white tutelage.

Such ideas gained wide acceptance among the European ruling classes and provided a convenient rationalization for the subjugation and exploitation of nonwhite peoples in the world. White adventurer Cecil Rhodes wrote to a friend in 1891: "I contend that we are the first race in the world, and that the more of the world we inhabit the better it is for the human race."

Around the same period, British colonial secretary Joseph Chamberlain stated, "The spirit of adventure and enterprise distinguishing the Anglo-Saxon race has made us peculiarly fit to carry out the working of colonization."

THE WHITE MAN'S BURDEN

Colonialism was rationalized as a manifestation of the Christian obligation to civilize backward peoples. Lord Frederick Lugard, who served as the first colonial governor of Nigeria, from 1912 to 1919, provided one of the most famous descriptions of the so-called white man's burden (that is, the duty of Europeans to bring civilization and progress to other cultures). In his book *The Dual Mandate in British Tropical Africa*, published in 1922, Lugard wrote that the passing away of the "picturesque methods of the past" may seem regrettable, but Europe had nevertheless brought progress to Africa. "[W]e must admit that the locomotive is a substantial improvement on head borne transport, and the modern van is more efficient than the camel," Lugard stated.

Colonialism brought the mind and method of Europe to bear on the people of Africa, and most Europeans believed this was a development for which Africans should have been grateful. Lugard stated, "At no time in the world's history has there been so cordial a hand held out to Africa . . . or a keener desire to assist the African in the path of progress." Lugard acclaimed colonialism as a civilizing mission: "Our present task is clear. It is to promote the commercial and industrial progress of Africa, without too careful a scrutiny of the material gains to ourselves."

GEOGRAPHICAL AND ENVIRONMENTAL DIFFERENCES

Most historians, scientists, economists, and scholars believe that people from Europe were able to colonize and dominate the 19th century world because of differences in the geography and environment of the two continents, not because of racial or ethnic differences. One of the leading exponents of this theory is Jared Diamond, whose book *Guns, Germs and Steel*, published in 1997, has helped change the way people think about history. According to Diamond, four factors are responsible for all historical developments: (1) the availability of potential crops and domestic animals, (2) the orientation of the continental axis to facilitate the spread of agriculture, (3) the transfer of knowledge between continents, and (4) population size.

British diplomat Frederick John Dealtry Lugard, who governed Nigeria from 1912 to 1919, is credited with developing Great Britain's policy of indirect rule—that is, the system of governing colonies through their traditional native institutions. This 1934 photograph shows Lord Lugard with a group of West African chiefs in London.

Diamond argued that the long east-west axis of Eurasia gave the continent's inhabitants a big advantage over the people living in the predominantly north-south landmasses of Africa, North America, and South America. Compared with Europe, Africa had far fewer indigenous crops and animals that could be domesticated. These factors hampered the development of farming. In addition, Africa's population was sparse and grouped in small and isolated communities, which limited the incentive for innovation. Researchers estimate that in 1500 Africa's total population was less than 50 million, which was less than that of Western Europe. Between 1700 and 1870 Europe's population more than doubled, while Africa's increased by only about 50 percent.

CULTURAL DIFFERENCES

Other theorists have emphasized differences in the cultural outlook of Europeans and of Africans. By the end of the Middle Ages (around the 15th century), people in Western Europe had begun to look upon nature as something to be tamed. They believed that humans had the capacity to control their physical environment and harness the powers of natural forces to serve their material needs. Europeans looked on technological innovations as the means to overcome the obstacles of nature and aid human progress. In contrast, until the arrival of Europeans, peoples in other parts of world still resigned themselves to the limitations imposed by their environment. African civilizations sought to harmonize themselves with nature and even worshipped aspects of it.

Economists have also stressed the importance of institutions in the growth of prosperity in Europe and its western offshoots. In his book *The Birth of Plenty: How the Prosperity of the World Was Created*, William Bernstein argues that four major institutions placed Europe ahead of other parts of the world: property rights, scientific rationalism, capital markets, and transportation/communication. According to Bernstein there was little economic growth anywhere in the world from the dawn of recorded history until 1820, when these four factors fell into place in Western Europe to create a formula for human material progress. Precolonial African societies lacked all four factors identified by Bernstein as underpinning the growth in wealth. However, the four institutions came together in Western European nations within the context of the Industrial Revolution and the growth of capitalism.

Before the Industrial Revolution there was little to separate Europe and Africa in terms of economic production. According to estimates in Angus Maddison's book *The World Economy: A*

Millennial Perspective, around 1000 A.D. the gross domestic product per capita (GDP, an economic indicator measuring annual individual earnings) was lower in Western Europe than it was in Africa. By 1500 Europe had overtaken Africa, with the income levels at $774 for Europe and $400 for Africa. The differences between the two regions continued to increase so that by 1820 Europe's GDP was $1,232, compared with Africa's $418. However, this gap of 3 to 1 was still small compared with 6 to 1 in 1913 and 13 to 1 by the year 2000.

NATIONALISM AND INDEPENDENCE MOVEMENTS

In the mid-1800s, large communities of Africans lived Western European lifestyles in settlements located in Sierra Leone, Liberia, Cape Coast (Gold Coast), and southern Nigeria. Among the residents were prosperous merchants and a variety of professionals such as doctors and teachers. Some were so successful that they could afford to send their children to Europe for education. These middle-class Africans were culturally quite different from ordinary Africans living within the continent's interior. It was from this minority of Westernized Africans that African political and cultural nationalism sprang.

(Opposite) Two indigenous men of Liberia pose in their native African garb. During the 1800s most educated middle-class blacks in Africa did not identify with their traditional culture, but emulated Western institutions and culture instead.

REJECTION OF AFRICAN CULTURE

Most of these middle-class Africans disapproved of their traditional culture. Some were as contemptuous of it as were ethnocentric whites. The liberated slaves who had left the Americas or Europe to settle in Africa did so not because they rejected Western civilization but because they had experienced racism. When they landed on Africa's shores, they did not fling off their Western clothes for native dress or abandon their slave names or do anything else to embrace the native culture. Instead, they held firmly to every cultural trait acquired in the Americas or Western Europe.

The detachment of these newcomers from native African communities may have been partly due to the fact that they originated from different parts of Africa. As such, many were strangers to the lands in which they settled. They may have also felt deep contempt for the African rulers who had sold them or their parents into slavery. Regardless of their reason for such alienation, they strongly preferred Western civilization over African ones. There was no doubt in their minds that Africa's future lay with emulating the West.

EARLY AFRICAN NATIONALISM

One of the most distinguished proponents of the Westernization of African culture was James Africanus Horton (1935–1883), a Creole born in Sierra Leone in 1835. Horton, whose parents were Igbos from eastern Nigeria, studied at King's College in London and Edinburgh University, where he completed his medical degree. Horton subsequently served as an officer in British army's medical service in West Africa, retiring as a lieutenant colonel around 1880.

Considered an early nationalist, Horton wrote several books in which he called for the education of Africans and for the establishment of independent West African nations. In his writings, however, Horton completely welcomed the Western influence in Africa, stating, "I, amongst a great many others, appreciate every European element that enters western Africa, whether in the capacity of merchants or pioneers of civilization, or in that of missionaries."

Horton hated many aspects of traditional African culture and believed that for much of the past millennium Africans had lived in darkness and ignorance. Although he urged Africans to copy European civilization, Horton did oppose white racism and claims that Africans were inherently inferior and incapable of development. Civilizations, he said, are subject to cyclic movements of progression and degeneration. He believed that Africa had had its time of greatness and progress centuries earlier, when it was a center of learning and literature. However, he theorized, Africans had eventually been overtaken by other races and as a result of stagnation, invasion, and slavery the continent had declined. Now Europe, which had languished in barbarism at the time of Africa's greatness, was at the height of civilization. Like many of his contemporaries, Horton believed that Africa's salvation rested in modernization and industrialization, not only of its economy but also of its institutions and culture.

DEFENDER OF AFRICAN CIVILIZATION

One of the strongest to disagree with the emulation of European culture was Edward Wilmot Blyden (1832–1912). Born in the Danish West-Indies, Blyden arrived in Monrovia in 1851 at the age of 18, after being prevented from entering a theological college in the United States because of his race. During the later half of the 19th century, Blyden became highly educated and wrote extensively on African history and culture. In West Africa he established a distinguished career as a politician, diplomat, and educator.

Proud of his race, Blyden condemned the ethnocentrism of European missionaries in Africa. He urged the African people to retain the essential characteristics of their unique African personality and society. In 1872, more than a decade before Europe's Scramble for Africa, Blyden called for a "spiritual decolonization," by asking Africa's coastal elites to shake off their spiritual bondage to European culture. (Decolonization refers to the process in which a colony becomes independent from a colonial power.)

Instead of emulating Europeans, Blyden insisted, Africans needed to follow their own true nature. In addition, he said, it was wrong for Europeans to presume that all races move along the same course of progress and that Africans are uncivilized and backward. Blyden believed that Africa had a socioeconomic system that was as advanced as anything in Europe. He saw traditional African society as essentially socialist, because it did not feature private ownership of property or businesses, but instead involved collective or government ownership.

As Blyden saw it, traditional Africa is classless, communitarian, and egalitarian. The extended family formed the foundation of a structure that incorporated common ownership of land, a communistic approach to work and distribution, and a

Born in the Virgin Islands of the Caribbean, Edward Wilmot Blyden immigrated to the African-American colony of Liberia as a young man. In his writings and speeches, Blyden promoted the idea that the natural culture of indigenous Africa was superior to that of the materialistic world of Europe and the United States. As one of Africa's first nationalists, Blyden supported the establishment of a modern West African state.

democratic political system. In Blyden's worldview Africans represented the antithesis of Europeans, whom he portrayed as harsh, individualistic, competitive, combative, highly materialistic, and lacking in faith, except in their ability to meddle with nature through science and industry.

Although Blyden believed that traditional Africans were morally superior to Europeans, he did not reject colonialism or the importation of the material products of Western civilization. He welcomed colonialism as a temporary means to bring Africa into the modern world. He believed that Africans needed to acquire Western technology, but that the science should be adapted to Africa's own needs and culture.

Blyden did, however, oppose the development of capitalism in Africa. He scorned the attempts by Westernized ex-slaves to develop free enterprise in the coastal settlements. Such ventures would inevitably fail, he said, because they ran against the grain of the African genius. According to Blyden, Africa did not need modern industries because it could exchange its raw materials with Western nations for manufactured goods. Similarly, Africa did not need to concern itself with developing science and technology.

Blyden's vision of Africa's future was consistent with the prevailing Western European ideas of free trade and the complementary nature of world economies. That is, Western industrializing nations were to serve as manufacturers of goods and the rest of world as suppliers of raw materials.

PAN-AFRICANISM AND CULTURAL NATIONALISM

Blyden was one of the first advocates of the concept of pan-Africanism—the idea that Africans are united in culture. He believed in the need for the development of an African consciousness—a feeling of oneness among the various peoples of the continent. This attitude was necessary, he explained, in order to strengthen the black race and reduce conflicts among its different nations. "An African nationality is our great need . . . we shall never receive the respect of other races until we establish a powerful nationality," Blyden said. He did not necessary envisage the creation of a single African state, although he actively sought the formation of one vast West African nation-state.

Blyden's cultural nationalist ideas influenced many subsequent nationalists in West Africa, including the Yoruba Baptist leader Pastor Mojola Agbebi (1860-1917). Agbebi was an avid black nationalist who fought for the establishment of an independent nondenominational African Church. An uncompromising defender of traditional African customs and institutions, Agbebi denounced European Christianity and called for Africanization of the religion.

The cultural nationalism of people like Blyden and Agbebi was in part a response to the racism of Europeans, who scorned African institutions and customs. It was also a challenge to the pro-Western stance of the African elites living along the West African coast. Blyden's brand of cultural nationalism, with its image of native Africans "leading a blameless and protracted existence and producing in their sequestered, beautiful, and futile home" would influence future generations of African nationalists.

EARLY POLITICAL ORGANIZATIONS

Under colonial rule, Africans had no rights as citizens, although they were often taxed or fined according to the government's laws. Many were subjected to forced labor, in which they suffered arbitrary punishments such whippings, imprisonment, and even death.

Diamond miners labor at the Wesselton Mines in Kimberley, South Africa, in this 1911 photograph. The treatment of the black workforce was one of many issues that led to the founding of political organizations fighting for African rights during the early 20th century.

As Africa's educated urban minority grappled with colonialism's racial and political impact on the people of the continent, many Africans formed political organizations in efforts to bring about change in the government. Early political organizations established in West Africa included the Aborigines Rights Protection Society in the Gold Coast, which was founded in 1897, and the People's Union, which was established in Nigeria in 1908. In Southern Africa the South African Native National Congress emerged in 1912, with the purpose to unite the African people and bring about political, social, and economic change. The group later became known as the ANC, or African National Congress.

INFLUENCE OF THE AFRICAN DIASPORA ON POLITICAL NATIONALISM

Black intellectuals and activists living outside the continent, in the African diaspora—particularly those living in countries such as the United States and the Caribbean—played a significant role in the development and growth of African nationalism. Indeed, it is widely thought that the concept of pan-Africanism originated in the New World. In the early days of African nationalism the view of Africa as a nation, with socioeconomic and political issues that needed to be addressed as a continent rather than as individual regions or countries, was more prevalent among the African diaspora than among those in Africa itself.

Black people living with racism in the Western Europe and the Americas were more likely to consider race as the source of their identity. As a result they were more likely to think of Africa as a single homeland for black people than were the actual inhabitants of the continent. In Africa, people defined themselves in relation to their families and larger communities. In Western Europe and the Americas, few of the descendants of African slaves had any idea where their ancestors had come from in Africa. Ties with their homelands had long been severed. “Africans in the Diaspora tend to look to Africa as one united continent, one unit,” explained African-American scholar W. E. B. Du Bois, “mainly because they cannot trace their particular roots.”

PAN-AFRICAN MOVEMENT

One of the major forces for pan-Africanism within the African diaspora was a London-educated barrister named Henry Sylvester Williams, who had been born on the Caribbean island of Trinidad. In 1900 he organized a meeting to discuss the worldwide situation of black people. The Pan-African Conference convened in London that same year, becoming the first meeting to address pan-African issues. At the conference, delegates protested against the theft of African lands by colonialists, racial discrimination, and other issues of interest to black people around the world.

W. E. B. Du Bois, who attended the 1900 conference, subsequently took over the leadership in the pan-African movement, organizing a series Pan-African Congresses held in Western European cities and the United States. At Congresses held between 1919 and 1945, members discussed the condition of Africans, demanded an end to racial subjugation, and advocated for gradual self-government in Africa. Members of the North

American-born William Edward Burghardt Du Bois organized a series of Pan-African Congresses to help bring attention to the racial discrimination and second-class citizenship status endured by blacks around the world. The first of five Pan-African Congresses organized by Du Bois took place in 1919.

American and Caribbean black intelligentsia made up the bulk of participants in these Congresses. Most of them accepted the idea that Western Europeans were performing a civilizing mission in Africa. Any criticisms of colonialism referred mainly to the exploitation of African lands and peoples, the brutal treatment of the natives, and the reluctance of the colonial authorities to educate their subjects.

The first Pan-African Congress, held in Paris in 1919, followed the end of the First World War. At that time W. E. B. Du Bois proposed the creation of a united African state, with its nucleus formed by the colonies taken from Germany following its defeat in the war. Du Bois suggested that the colonies administered by Portugal and Belgium be added to the proposed new state since these European nations had shown a lack of ability to fairly govern colonial people. Eventually all southern Africa, except the Union of South Africa, should be included in the new African state, explained Du Bois. He did not envisage the new state as independent and self-governing at first, but under international control.

The creation of an African state would not involve the migration of the African diaspora back to Africa, wrote Du Bois, since black people had earned the right to fight for equality in the New World. Rather the service that the Westernized African diaspora would be expected to perform would be to provide, from time to time, technical expertise and leaders of thought and missionaries of culture to help develop the new nation. In his vision of an

African State apparently Du Bois assumed the superiority of the Western culture over that of the indigenous African culture.

MARCUS GARVEY AND THE "BACK TO AFRICA" MOVEMENT

A more radical influence on African nationalism in the early 20th century was the Jamaican-born nationalist Marcus Garvey. Garvey was one of the most influential, and controversial, black leaders in the 20th century. In 1914 he founded the Universal Negro Improvement Association (UNIA), which advocated worldwide black unity and an end to colonialism. By the 1920s Garvey, a brilliant tactician and master of propaganda, had millions of followers.

Another nationalist in the African diaspora was Marcus Garvey, who advocated an end to colonialism and called for educated blacks to move back to Africa to protect the continent from further imperialism. Founder of the Universal Negro Improvement Association, Garvey believed in developing economic and political opportunities for black communities worldwide.

Garvey promoted race pride among black people and fervently opposed integration with other races, particularly whites. He strongly identified with Africa and campaigned that the continent belonged to Africans. One of his dreams was the establishment of an autonomous African republic free from white domination. In 1916 Garvey moved from Jamaica to the United States and set up a steamship company, the Black Star, as part of his Back to Africa movement, which promoted the idea that people of African ancestry should return to their homeland. Many historians today believe that Garvey never intended a mass exodus of blacks to Africa, as is commonly assumed. What he desired was the return of some skilled and educated blacks to help indigenous Africans develop a strong nation powerful enough to advance the interests of black people throughout the world and compel the respect of other nations.

Perhaps one of the more significant contributions made by Garvey to the development of African nationalism was his uncompromising insistence on the need for African nationhood and independence. In a period when most black nationalists were demanding gradual self-government for Africans, Garvey's demand for immediate political freedom for all colonized peoples and his rejection of the colonialist concept of tutelage made a considerable impression on young African nationalists.

RADICALIZING PERIOD

By 1940 almost every territory on the continent of Africa had nationalist groups working for rights of black Africans. Many of the men and women serving as leaders of these independence movements had been radicalized while living in Western Europe or the United States, mainly as students, during the period leading to the Second World War (1939–1945) and shortly after. This was a time when Europe was in political and economic turmoil, and the imperial powers appeared vulnerable.

During World War II several African nations, including South Africa, Nigeria, Kenya, and Tanganyika, joined forces with the Allies (the United Kingdom, France, the United States, and others) against the Axis Powers (Germany, Italy, Japan, and others). The experience of fighting on the side of the Allied forces for the cause of freedom made many Africans and other colonial subjects politically aware of their own lack of civil rights. This enlightenment was succinctly expressed in a message that a Nigerian soldier expressed in a letter home from India in 1945. He wrote: "We overseas soldiers are coming back home with new ideas. We have been told what we fought for, that is freedom. We want freedom, nothing but freedom."

African students from various parts of Africa who studied in Western Europe or the Americas also had opportunities to meet and discuss their experiences with colonialism with each other. These interactions served to cultivate and strengthen the African nationalist perspective among young Africans who were later to make up the vanguard of the independence movements.

ETHNIC NATIONALISM

The pre-independence era saw not only the growth of African nationalism but also the development of ethnic nationalism. Arguably the strongest identities that emerged during this period were based on ethnicity, not continental ancestry. Many African nationalist leaders were also ethnic leaders. For example, Jomo Kenyatta, while supporting pan-Africanism, promoted Kikuyu nationalism in Kenya.

Ethnic nationalism grew during colonial rule partly in response to the forced unification of various ethnic groups within the artificial boundaries that had been established by Europeans unfamiliar with the populations they ruled. Before colonial rule, most kingdoms in Africa operated as autonomous political entities, in which the inhabitants identified themselves according to where they lived. For example, before the 19th century there was no common Yoruba identity or Igbo nationality. The term Yoruba originally referred solely to people of the Oyo kingdom.

Eventually, as intercommunal migration and trade developed among people living in Oyo and the surrounding kingdoms of Egba, Ijebu, Ekiti, and Ibadan, an ethnic identity evolved. Because they shared the same language and belief in a common ancestry, the people developed a common identity as Yorubas. Individual ethnic identities strengthened as African cities grew in size, and people from various communities within the same ethnic group could meet. Similarly, students from similar ethnic backgrounds interacted and formed bonds while studying abroad. For instance, it was in London that Egbe Omo Oduduwa formed the first pan-Yoruba organization, in 1945.

THE 1945 PAN-AFRICAN CONGRESS

The increased political consciousness among African students and migrants living abroad was evident at the fifth Pan-African Congress, held in Manchester, England, in 1945. Unlike the previous Congresses, which had been dominated by the African diaspora, this meeting was attended by a large number of Africans from Africa. Among them were future political leaders: Kwame Nkrumah from the Gold Coast, Jomo Kenyatta from Kenya, Obafemi Awoslowo from Nigeria, and Hastings Banda from Malawi. The Congress also included W. E. B. Du Bois and Mrs. Amy Garvey, the widow of Marcus Garvey.

In contrast to the politically moderate approach of the previous meetings, the fifth Congress called for speedy decolonization and warned that failure to grant freedom to the colonies could trigger wars of liberation. The Congress's "Declaration to the Colonial and subject peoples of the World," written by Kwame Nkrumah, stated:

> We believe in the rights of all peoples to govern themselves. We affirm the right of all colonial peoples to control their own destiny. All colonies must be free from foreign imperialist control, whether political or economic. The peoples of the colonies must have the right to elect their own government, a government without restrictions from a foreign power. We say to the peoples of the colonies that they must strive for these ends by all means at their disposal. . . . Today there is only one road to effective action—the organisation of the masses. Colonial and subject peoples of the world—unite!

RESISTANCE TO COLONIALISM

During the 1930s and 1940s many nationalists looked at Ethiopia as a symbol for African power and resistance to colonial rule. In

Picture Post, November 10, 1945

The Abyssinian Delegate
Jomo Kenyatta asked for an Act of Parliament making discrimination by race or colour a criminal offence.

The Nigerian Trade Unionist
Chief A. S. Coker, represents unions with a membership of half a million workers. He demands full franchise for the negro worker.

The Liverpool Welfare Worker
Mr. E. J. Du Plau, is responsible for hostels and centres for negro seamen. "Negroes are social exiles in Britain," he maintains.

AFRICA SPEAKS IN MANCHESTER

Delegates from many parts of Africa and the United States to the first Pan-African Conference talk for a week—of freedom from the White Man, of the colour bar, of one great coloured nation, of force to gain their ends.

Photographed by JOHN DEAKIN

THE dance was a mixed affair—mixed in trade, from the stoker to the anthropologist; mixed in class, from the £3 a week labourer to the rich cocoa merchant; mixed in dress, from the baggy grey flannels to the suit of tails. But above all it was mixed in colour, from the blonde white to the midnight black. This dance, held at Edinburgh Hall, on the corner of one of Manchester's drab and soot-blackened streets, was the first gathering of delegates to the Pan-African Conference. They chose Manchester because its people have less curiosity or hostility to colour than the people of any other English city. Certainly, there was no self-consciousness among the white women who partnered their negro husbands or friends through "jive" to the last romantic waltz. Their attitudes varied. Some had approached the colour bar problem intellectually, others from a Christian viewpoint and others from simple human values.

Typical of the last attitude is the mixed marriage of Mary Brown to John Teah Brown, and before the conference got down to the more serious problems of the negro peoples, I went to their home to see a successful black and white marriage in its own domestic setting. Mary Brown was left stranded in Liverpool with her child when she met John Brown, a donkeyman on a merchant ship. He married her, gave her overwhelming affection, and saw that her child was properly educated.

I listened to John Teah Brown's story—a story which in many ways put in terms of one human being the resolutions and speeches of the whole week's conference. John Teah Brown was born in Sierre Leone and is a member of the Kroo tribe. He was educated at a mission and brought up a Roman Catholic. He was devout and sincere in his religion until one day in a church at East London, South Africa. He went in to pray but a priest came up to him and told him it was a white man's church and he must get out. He has not been inside a church since, though he remains true to the Christian faith, practising it, he thinks, with rather more sincerity than the priest who turned him away from the altar.

He left Sierra Leone at the age of fifteen, for he

Continued overleaf

A Mixed Marriage That is a Success
Mr. John Teah Brown, with his white wife, Mrs. Mary Brown, in their Manchester home. He says the negro must earn the respect of the white man to merit full citizenship.

19

Newspaper coverage of the Pan-African Congress held in Manchester, England, in 1945. Many of the attendees would later become leaders of newly independent nations in Africa.

1930 an Ethiopian nobleman named Tafari Makonnen had been crowned emperor, and called Haile Selassie. Six years later Italy invaded the country, and Selassie joined Ethiopian fighters in defending the country. Although he and his forces were defeated and Italy declared Ethiopia an Italian colony, Selassie took his case to the General Assembly of the League of Nations. The international organization had been formed after the First World War to address grievances among its member states in a legal forum.

In an eloquent speech, Selassie accused the Italians of engaging in unethical warfare, including the use of chemical weapons and other actions counter to the rules of war as established by the Geneva Convention. Although his words won him worldwide attention, Selassie did not succeed in regaining his throne for several more years. After he reclaimed the throne in Ethiopia in 1941, he continued to serve as a rare example of an African nation governed by an African.

Another African leader who challenged Europeans came to power in Egypt in 1954. Although independent from Britain since 1922, Egypt had remained under control of British interests under a constitutional monarchy. In 1952 Colonel Gamal Abdel Nasser led a military coup against the British-backed rule of King Farouk I, who was known for his lavish lifestyle and corrupt regime. Two years later Nasser forced the first president of the Republic of Egypt, General Muhammad Naguib, from power and became a military dictator over Egypt. When Nasser nationalized the Suez Canal in 1956, his action led Britain, France, and Israel to invade. UN intervention helped alleviate the crisis, and Nasser became a hero to many Egyptians because he was seen as having freed the country from European domination.

In Kenya, grievances over British colonial rule had led to the founding in 1944 of the Kenya African Union (KAU), led by nationalist leader Jomo Kenyatta. Soon after, the Kikuyu people began protesting over the loss of agricultural and grazing land set

Following Ethiopia's defeat during the Second Italo-Abyssinian War (1935–36), Emperor Haile Selassie argued before the League of Nations against the right of Italy to take his nation as a colony. The League was unable to help Selassie reclaim his throne, although he assumed leadership again in 1941, when Ethiopia was liberated during World War II.

aside by the British for the exclusive use of white farmers. The first uprising occurred in 1952, and efforts by the colonial authorities to crush it led to a large-scale war. Much of the resistance to colonial rule came from the efforts of a secret organization known as the Mau Mau.

The British cracked down on the Mau Mau rebellions, imposing a state of emergency in Kenya that lasted until 1959. Some historians believe that the Mau Mau rebellion against the British colonialists in Kenya in the 1950s was largely the result of the growth in Kikuyu nationalism rather than a manifestation of Kenyan nationalism. Regardless, the anticolonial violence in Kenya led Britain to give in to calls for political change in Africa.

POST-COLONIAL AFRICA

In 1958 a Pan-African Congress took place on African soil for the first time. It was held in the city of Accra, in the newly renamed Gold Coast. The country was now called Ghana, after the great 11th century African empire that had once thrived several hundred miles to the north. A former British colony, Ghana had become the first nation of colonial sub-Saharan Africa to gain independence, in 1957. Following elections held in 1960, anticolonial-rule leader Kwame Nkrumah became the new country's first president.

(Opposite) In March 1957 the new Ghanaian prime minister Kwame Nkrumah waves to crowds at the Assembly House in Accra, where the independence of Ghana was formally declared. In the decade that followed, many more African nations threw off the yoke of colonial rule.

ACHIEVING POLITICAL INDEPENDENCE

Many colonies in West Africa gained independence during the 1960s. Among them were the former British colonies of Nigeria (1960), Sierra Leone (1961), and The Gambia (1965).

In 1960 most French colonies and two French trust territories (Cameroon and Togo) became independent states through peaceful

transition. They were Dahomey (later called Benin), Niger, Upper Volta (later renamed Burkina Faso), Côte d'Ivoire, Chad, the Central African Republic, the French Congo (Brazzaville), Gabon, Senegal, Mali, and Mauritania. France remained strongly involved with these colonies and continued to provide a range of financial and technological assistance and control over their industry, banking, and trade institutions.

One French colony, however refused to remain aligned with France—in 1958 Guinea voted against approval of the constitution of the French Community, an action that essentially broke its ties with France. The new state was governed by President Ahmed Sékou Touré.

In the French colony of Algeria, independence came after years of warfare that had begun in 1954. In 1962, the leader of the National Liberation Front (FLN), Ahmed Ben Bella, claimed victory over France. Afterward, most European settlers and their descendants fled the country, and Ahmed Ben Bella assumed the role of prime minister of Algeria's provisional government before becoming the newly independent country's first president.

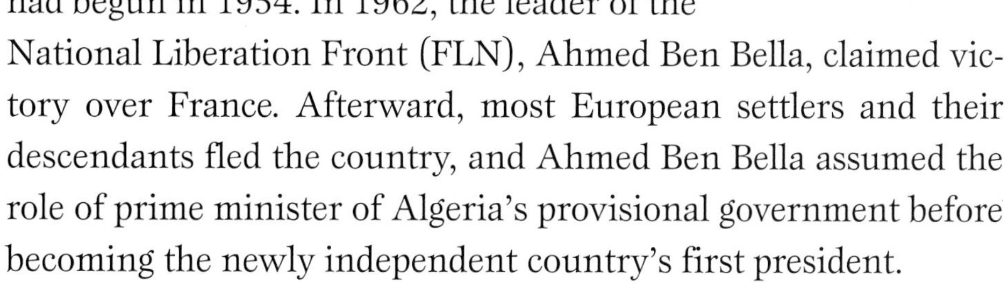

The violence of the Mau Mau uprisings during the 1950s in Kenya helped convince the British to grant independence to several of its former colonies in eastern and central Africa during the 1960s. In 1961, Tanganyika achieved independence, then three years later united with Zanzibar (which gained independence in 1963), forming the United Republic of Tanzania. Kenya followed in 1963, with nationalist leader Jomo Kenyatta elected as prime minister in the nation's first multiracial elections held

In New York City, in October 1962, Prime Minister Ahmed Ben Bella (left) confers with members of the Algerian delegation at the United Nations, which the newly independent nation had just joined. The following year Bella became the first president of the People's Democratic Republic of Algeria.

that year. In 1964 Nyasaland gained independence as Malawi, and Northern Rhodesia became Zambia.

The Belgian Congo, with its turbulent history as King Leopold's Congo Free State was granted independence in 1960. Charismatic nationalist leader Patrice Lumumba assumed the role of prime minister for the newly independent nation, although he would be assassinated the following year.

AFRICAN SOCIALISM

Most of the first generation post-independence African leaders professed some form of African socialism as their creed. These African socialists considered the traditional African society as a form of socialism—a society that was classless and communal, and in which land belonged to the community. In traditional African culture, socialists explained, the concept of private ownership of property did not exist.

African socialists also considered the traditional African political system as one founded on the principle of democracy. For example, Africans would traditionally settle differences by holding a "palaver"—a discussion in which everyone was allowed to express an opinion, and then the majority opinion provided the decision. African socialists were also pan-African, believing in the essential unity of Africans and the existence of an African culture and personality.

African socialists, like earlier nationalists, did not reject the material products and creations of western civilization. They wanted to marry western technology with traditional structures and values to produce a new civilization. Tanzania founding president, Julius Nyerere, explained:

> Our problem is just this—how to get the benefits of European society—benefits which have been brought by an organization of society based on an exaggerated ideal of the rights of individuals—and yet retain the African's own structure of society in which the individual is a member of a kind of fellowship.

As African socialists saw it, their socialist model of development promised modernization and industrialization without the destructive consequences associated with the capitalist system of the West. In the early 1960s, African socialist thinking was given some credence and encouragement by Western liberals in search of an alternative to capitalism. But it soon became clear that Africa was not the source of a new ideology of human advancement.

In reality, much of African socialism was based on myths about the nature of the indigenous traditional culture. As Nkrumah admitted in the 1960s, "an idyllic African classless society (in which there were no rich and no poor) enjoying a drugged serenity is certainly a facile simplification."

In addition, the socialist ideology provided little in the way of any practical guide for Africans faced with enormous challenges of developing their new nations. In fact, some Africans later came to believe that the customs associated with African traditional culture may actually have hindered the continent's modern economic and social development. For example, the traditional customs of giving and taking "presents" within an extended family, Nkrumah wrote in his book *Africa Must Unite*, "encourage indolence and bribery, they act as a brake upon ability, they discourage that deeper sense of individual responsibility which must be ready in a period of active reconstruction to accept obligation and fulfill trust." Because this cultural attitude facilitated bribery and corruption, it hindered productivity and slowed development in Africa, he explained.

Nevertheless, socialism was embraced by many new African leaders. They established socialist economic policies, such as the nationalization (government takeover) of agricultural and industrial businesses. Both Nkrumah, in Ghana, and Ahmed Sékou Touré, in Guinea, established socialist governments based on the philosophy of the communist philosopher Karl Marx. Many leaders of the new African states also turned their countries into one-party states, effectively suppressing political opposition and expression.

ORGANIZATION OF AFRICAN UNITY

During the 1960s the concept of a united Africa took shape in the form of the Organization of African Unity (OAU), a group of African heads of state. Founded in 1963, the OAU merged two ideological rival blocs that were known as the Casablanca and Monrovia groups, into which Africa's 32 independent states had divided. The division stemmed mainly from differences in ideology and commitment to African unity.

The Casablanca group, which included Algeria, Egypt, Ghana, Guinea, and Morocco, held a more radical perspective on

African unity and decolonization. It argued for pan-African political unity through the creation of an African organization with shared structures and institutions (including a common economic market), African citizenship, and an African military command. The Monrovia group, which included Nigeria and Liberia, was more moderate. The faction included the majority of independent states, which were not keen on political integration, but preferred the gradual formation of a united economic structure. The Monrovia group's representatives also insisted on the principle of non-interference in the affairs of states.

Many of the leaders in the Casablanca camp were more fervent in their opposition to Western imperialism and less willing to maintain special ties with their former colonial masters than their moderate colleagues. Nkrumah of Ghana went so far as to

Founded in 1963 and based in Addis Ababa, Ethiopia, the Organization of African Unity (OAU) fostered pan-Africanism by bringing together member states to discuss issues affecting the entire continent. However, the OAU charter stipulated that states not interfere with each other's internal affairs, reducing the effectiveness of the organization.

propose the formation of a continental army to liberate African territories still under colonial or white-minority government rule. The radical stance of Gamal Abdel Nasser of Egypt was apparent from his past actions: he had nationalized the Suez Canal in 1956, precipitating a short-lived invasion by Britain, France, and Israel. (Nasser was both a pan-Arabist and an advocate of pan-Africanism.) The Algerian leader, Ben Bella, was the revolutionary leader who had led his country in a war of independence against France. Another radical leader of the Casablanca camp was the Guinean Marxist ruler Ahmed Sékou Touré, who in 1958 had led Guinea out of the French Community by encouraging the people of Guinea to vote for complete independence from France in a national referendum.

Nigeria was a leading force in the Monrovia group. The country's government was among the most conservative in the continent. In his speech to mark Nigeria's independence in 1960, the new prime minister, Abubakar Tafawa Balewa, thanked the British for their "devotion" in developing Nigeria "first as masters, then as leaders, finally as partners, but always as friends." Some people viewed the statements as deferential to the British and defensive of colonialism. Most former French West African states also supported the Monrovia group, because they favored close relations with former colonial powers, particularly France.

The creation of the OAU was largely due to the efforts of Ethiopian ruler Haile Selassie, who mediated a compromise between the Monrovia and Casablanca groups. The resulting organization reflected much more of the vision of the moderate African states than that of the radical ones. Ultimately its purpose, as stated in its charter, was to facilitate cooperation between equal and sovereign states. Its intention was not to provide a means for the economic or political integration of African nations. The charter included a clause that stipulated that member states could not interfere in each other's internal affairs.

WHITE-MINORITY RULE

In several colonies, white-minority governments maintained control during decolonization. These governments rejected any idea of African majority rule and in many cases banned African nationalist political organizations.

In the British colony of South Africa, Afrikaner Nationalists, whose members believed in the superiority of whites over blacks, came to power in 1948. The party subsequently imposed a racial rule in South Africa called apartheid. The system segregated blacks and whites in every part of life: home, work, education, public services, and politics.

In 1952 black nationalists in the African National Congress began a "Defiance Campaign" to protest against apartheid laws. The ANC asked volunteers to deliberately get arrested, thereby filling the courts and prisons in order to break down the system. One of the activists organizing the campaign was Nelson Mandela. In 1955 the ANC drew up a "Freedom Charter" that stated: "South Africa belongs to all who live in it, black and white." It also made demands that all citizens had the right to vote, hold office, and be equal before the law.

In 1959 the South African prime minister Hendrik Verwoerd announced plans for the creation of separate homelands for each ethnic group in the country. He announced that South Africa would become a "multinational" state with separate homelands for eight black "nations." Two years later, in 1961, his government declared the Republic of South Africa independent from Great Britain, under white-minority rule.

In March 1960 protests by another political group, the Pan-Africanist Congress (PAC), in the black township of Sharpeville, near the city of Johannesburg, resulted in the government massacre of almost 70 Africans. As a result world attitudes toward the South Africa government began to change. Verwoerd ordered

World support of the white-minority government ruling South Africa declined after the massacre at Sharpeville, a township outside Johannesburg. An estimated 70 black South Africans died on March 21, 1960, when police fired on Pan-Africanist Congress activists protesting against legislation that forced blacks to carry identity passes.

a massive crackdown on dissidents, which resulted in the imprisonment of thousands of anti-apartheid activists.

Although the ANC remained committed to nonviolence, one of its offshoot organizations, headed by anti-apartheid activist Nelson Mandela, committed to armed struggle. In July 1962 after being charged with inciting African workers to strike illegally and with leaving the country without a valid travel document, Mandela was sentenced to five years in prison. When information about his involvement with the armed guerrilla resistance emerged, the sentence was extended. At Mandela's trial on this charge, he made the following statement to the South African court:

> During my lifetime I have dedicated myself to this struggle of the African people. I have fought against white domination, and I have fought against black domination. I have cherished the ideal of a democratic and free society in which all persons live together in harmony and with equal opportunities. It is an ideal which I hope to live for and to achieve. But if needs be, it is an ideal for which I am prepared to die.

In June 1964, at the age of 45 years old, Nelson Mandela was sentenced to life imprisonment. He and eight other African National Congress leaders were jailed at Robben Island, South Africa, and the African nationalist movement was silenced.

In the Portuguese colony of Mozambique, black nationalists also resorted to violence and armed struggle. Nationalist groups united to form the Mozambique Liberation Front (FRELIMO) and engaged in guerrilla warfare until 1974, when the Portuguese government was overthrown by the military. The new government entered into talks with FRELIMO that resulted in a cease-fire, and the country became independent in 1975. Other Portuguese colonies that waged years of armed struggles before gaining political independence were Guinea–Bissau (in 1974) and Angola (in 1975).

In Rhodesia the white-minority government led by Prime Minister Ian Smith declared independence from the British Commonwealth in 1965, and for the next 14 years the country remained under white-minority rule. During that time the military wings of the Zimbabwe African National Union (ZANU, led by Robert Mugabe) and the Zimbabwe African People's Union (ZAPU, led by Joshua Nkomo) fought to end white rule. Both parties derived their names from the Great Zimbabwe Empire of southeastern Africa.

After years of warfare and the imposition of economic sanctions by other countries, the Rhodesian government agreed in 1979 to hold nonracial and democratic elections. However, the elections did not include the ZANU and ZAPU parties. A subsequent peace plan agreement led to internationally supervised elections in 1980, during which Robert Mugabe of the ZANU party was elected president of the newly named Republic of Zimbabwe.

MILITARY COUPS AND INTERNAL CONFLICTS

In many African countries, decolonization and the establishment of African-majority governments was quickly followed by internal strife. Soon after the colonists departed, the nation-states they bequeathed began to fall apart. In 1965 the socialist and dictatorial government of Algeria's president Ahmed Ben Bella was overthrown by his minister of defense, military leader Houari Boumédiènne. That same year saw General Joseph-Désiré Mobutu oust President Joseph Kasa-Vubu of the Congo. In 1966, Nigeria's civilian government fell, as did Nkrumah's government in Ghana and Haile Selassie's in Ethiopia. Within a decade of independence, about a third of the governments in Africa had been toppled in military coups.

Houari Boumédiènne was one of many African leaders who seized power in military coups that took place throughout Africa after former colonies achieved independence. In a bloodless coup in Algeria in 1965, Boumédiènne assumed the presidency and subsequently ruled the country until his death in 1978.

Various explanations have been given for the weakness of nation-states in Africa and their vulnerability to internal conflict. Some writers trace the problem back to colonialism. They believe the Berlin conference that apportioned Africa among European powers divided its peoples in such a way that future conflicts were inevitable. The "divide-and-conquer" tactics used by colonial powers to control their domains exacerbated rivalries between groups that were being forced to live together in colonies. Tensions among these groups led to instability in the newly formed independent states.

Some historians and political scientists have argued that the Western European political and economic institutions forced upon Africa during colonial rule were unworkable because they differed too much from the traditional structures of African civilizations. In particular, Western forms of democracy, it is said, were grafted on to societies that had very different social and political customs from those of Western Europe. Nevertheless, most African leaders came to value modern democratic institutions. Today, they generally agree that the political problems faced by most African nations since independence have stemmed from deficits in modern democratic culture rather than from too much democracy.

CAUSES OF CIVIL CONFLICTS

Civil strife in modern Africa has made it the most conflict-ridden region in the world today. Between 1960 and 2003, 107 African leaders were overthrown, two thirds of whom were killed, jailed, or driven into exile. Since the 1960s nearly 20 African countries (comprising about 40 percent of sub-Saharan Africa) have experienced at least one period of internal conflict, or civil war. Since 1960 more than 9 million people have perished in Africa's internal conflicts—far more than the number who died in political violence during almost a century of colonial rule.

Economists from the World Bank (an international organization that provides monetary and technical assistance to developing nations) have analyzed the causes of civil conflict in the world, especially in sub-Saharan Africa. They report that the main causes of internal strife can be described as greed, grievances, or a combination of both.

Greed leads to conflict when rebel groups lay claim to natural resources in a grab for personal riches. In such cases the conflict is instigated and prolonged mainly for the purpose of making a profit, commonly by stealing the nation's mineral resources. Rebels may manufacture grievances or adapt existing ones to legitimize such ventures.

A grievance is said to be a cause of conflict in cases where a group, usually an ethnic minority, is driven to rebellion because of oppression by a larger or stronger group that controls the state. Grievances can stem from any number of perceived injustices, such as economic inequality, political repression, and ethnic or religious persecution. For example, in the former Belgium protectorate of Rwanda, ethnic domination by the minority Tutsi upper class over the majority Hutu was a major factor in a conflict that led to the genocide of hundreds of thousands of Tutsis in 1994.

Most civil wars in Africa have had elements of both greed and grievances, but in more recent years greed appears to be the dominant factor. States that have been most affected by internal conflicts tend to be rich in mineral resources. The lure of natural wealth has encouraged local populations to attempt to break away from national governments, with rebel groups often operating out of regions rich in resources. During the early 1960s the province of Katanga (which is rich in cobalt, copper, tin, uranium, and diamonds) tried unsuccessfully to secede from the Congo. From 1967 to 1970 Nigerian government forces waged a civil war with secessionist Biafra, which has abundant oil resources. Since the late 1970s rebels in Angola have been fighting to make the oil-rich province of Cabinda a separate nation. Rebel groups commonly use the profits made from expropriating resources such as gold, copper, or diamonds to finance their operations.

Ethnic tensions resulting from decades of domination by the Tutsis over the Hutus have been blamed for the 1994 genocide in Rwanda. Within an hour of the April 6 plane crash that killed Rwandan President Juvenal Habyarimana, members of the Rwandan armed forces and extremist militia began an organized, systematic slaughter of Tutsis. Among the nearly 800,000 Rwandans who died were hundreds of Tutsis killed at the Rukara Catholic mission, in Rukara.

CIVIL WAR IN SUDAN

One of the longest-lasting civil wars of the 20th century has wracked the African nation of Sudan. Even before achieving independence from Great Britain in 1956, the country saw civil strife, in which non-Arab and non-Muslim Sudanese living in the south battled the Arab Muslims of the north for autonomy. That conflict, during which a half a million people died, lasted from 1955 to 1972, until it ended with the signing of the Addis Ababa Agreement.

A little more than a decade later, the second Sudanese civil war broke out, although it essentially was a continuation of the first war. Over the following two decades an estimated 2 million

ARMED CONFLICTS IN AFRICA

According to the *Project Ploughshares Armed Conflicts Report 2005* there were 14 armed conflicts in Africa in 2004, accounting for 44 percent of such conflicts in the world. These conflicts have not only resulted in large numbers of deaths but also brought misery to untold numbers of survivors. In 2004 approximately 15 million Africans were internally displaced, and around 4.5 million Africans sought refuge in neighboring countries.

civilians in southern Sudan died and more than 4 million were displaced. The conflict ended in January 2005 with the signing of the Naivasha peace treaty. However, a separate conflict that began in 2003 in the western region of Sudan, called Darfur, continues to take lives and displace millions of people.

COLD WAR INFLUENCE

After African countries gained independence, foreign powers commonly instigated political trouble and exacerbated existing rivalries within the new nations. In the former Portuguese colony of Angola, for example, two rival anticolonial liberation movements began fighting each other after the country gained independence in 1975. South Africa struck an alliance with one faction (União Nacional para a Independência Total de Angola, or UNITA) and invaded the country. Meanwhile, the Soviet Union and Cuba had established ties with another faction, Movimento Popular de Libertação de Angola, or MPLA. Their military and economic support helped the MPLA come to power.

The United States subsequently joined with South Africa to support UNITA, the faction fighting the MPLA government. As a result, the civil war in Angola became part of the ongoing Cold War (1947–1991), an ideological conflict in which capitalist countries, led by the United States, struggled against the communist bloc of nations, led by the Soviet Union.

By the 1990s Cold War ideology was no longer driving the fighting in Angola. Instead, greed was the cause of ongoing warfare as the MPLA and UNITA sought ownership over Angola's rich oil and diamond deposits. The civil war in Angola lasted from 1975 to 2002, and resulted in the death of as many as a million people.

The decades of antagonism between the United States and the Soviet Union affected many other developing nations in Africa. During the Cold War the two superpowers offered inducements to new governments to align with them. Once a government took a side, it became the target of subversive activities supported by the other superpower. A common way to destabilize a new nation was to fund and arm the ethnic-based rebel group fighting the established government.

After assuming power in the Belgian Congo in a military coup in 1965, General Joseph-Désiré Mobutu ruled the nation, which he renamed Zaire, for 32 years as undisputed dictator. Despite his reputation for brutality, Mobutu Sese Seko was supported by Western powers because of his anti-communist, pro-Western stance.

Cold War ideology had helped bring General Joseph-Désiré Mobutu to power in the Belgium Congo in 1965, during a military coup supported by the United States. He later called himself Mobutu Sese Seko, and as president of the newly named Zaire ran a regime of terror, corruption, and oppression. However, his pro-Western, anticommunist stance brought loans and military support that allowed him to remain in power for decades, until he was overthrown in 1997, during the First Congo War. At that time rebel leader Laurent

Kabila assumed leadership of the renamed Democratic Republic of the Congo.

SELF-DETERMINATION

A few African countries did not gain independence until the 1990s. Namibia, which had been occupied since World War I by South Africa, gained independence in 1990 after decades of guerrilla warfare. Eritrea broke away from Ethiopia in 1993 after 30 years of fighting. However, it was the goal of African majority rule and the battle against apartheid in South Africa that captured much of the world's attention during the 1990s.

In 1990 Nelson Mandela was released from prison just as the institutionalized racism of apartheid was beginning to collapse. The following year he was elected to head the African National Congress and in 1993 received the Nobel Peace Prize. In 1994, during the first nonracial elections ever held in South Africa, Nelson Mandela was elected president, bringing African-majority rule to the nation.

INEFFECTIVENESS OF THE OAU

Although the purpose of the OAU was to positively influence political and economic development in Africa, over the years the organization was widely criticized for its inability to do so. Its principle of non-interference in African states and its lack of a mechanism to influence the internal affairs of its members left it unable to settle wars, impose sanctions against erring nations, pressure oppressive rulers, or effectively promote economic unity.

OAU weakness could be seen in Uganda, where the brutal dictator Idi Amin came to power in a military coup in 1971. The organization remained silent during his regime, which lasted until 1979, while he killed tens of thousands of its opponents. The OAU also failed to condemn governments in other African

In April 1994 millions of South Africans stood in long lines to vote in their country's first nonracial, democratic elections. The following month saw Nelson Mandela take the oath of office in Pretoria, becoming South Africa's first black president.

countries that flagrantly violated their citizens' human rights. International and civil wars erupted and raged in various parts of Africa without any OAU intervention or efforts to mediate peace talks. However, the organization did adopt the African Charter on Human and People's Rights in 1981 and later established the African Rights Commission, located in Banjul, The Gambia.

The OAU was not very successful in promoting economic cooperation within the continent either. Over the course of three decades, African leaders passed numerous resolutions and adopted many plans to arrive at a common approach to economic development and to promote economic integration among African nations. The Lagos Plan of Action of 1980 called for incorporating programs and strategies for self-reliant development and cooperation among African countries. Africa's Priority Program for Economic Recovery, approved in 1985, was an emergency program meant to tackle the development crisis of the 1980s, in the wake of drought and famine that had engulfed the continent. In 1991 OAU members signed the Abuja Treaty, which established the African Economic Community, which seeks to create an economic union of African countries.

NEW PARTNERSHIP FOR AFRICA'S DEVELOPMENT

In 2001, in an effort to address the problems of growing poverty and underdevelopment in many African nations, the OAU adopted the New Partnership for Africa's Development (NEPAD). At that time 15 nations signed on to the program, which strives to provide a common platform for African governments and agencies to engage the international community in partnership. NEPAD calls on industrial nations to bridge the financial gap between what Africa has and what it needs to

At the end of the February 2004 summit of the New Partnership for Africa's Development (NEPAD), held in Kigali, Rwanda, African leaders pose for a group photo. At the meeting, members approved a peer review system for monitoring each other's governments in the areas of economic management, human rights, corruption, and democracy.

bring its infrastructure and formal institutions to levels necessary for strong economic growth and poverty eradication.

Under NEPAD African leaders have also committed to implement democracy reforms, including setting up an Africa Peer Review Mechanism, whereby the human rights records of member states are put under collective scrutiny. This move towards greater democracy reflects the recognition by African governments that they must improve governance, transparency, and stability in their respective nations. Such changes should encourage support from donors, international corporations, and others.

7 AFRICA TODAY

(Opposite) In July 2002 Libyan leader Muammar Gadhafi speaks during the ceremony marking the official launch of the African Union (AU). The new organization has greater powers than those of the OAU, such as the right to intervene in the internal affairs of member states in order to "restore peace and stability" and to "prevent war crimes, genocide and crimes against humanity."

The pan-African dream is still alive in the 21st century. Political leaders from all regions of Africa continue to champion African solidarity and aspire to uniting the peoples of the continent in a strong and purposeful state. However, not all Africans support the idea of a politically and economically unified Africa. Some are wary of programs that allow free trade, preferring that their governments protect local businesses and interests from outside competition.

THE AFRICAN UNION

In 2002, in an effort to accelerate the process of political and economic integration in the continent and to address the many political, social, and economic problems confronting African countries, members of the Organization of African Unity voted to replace the OAU with the African Union (AU). Hopeful that a new approach would accelerate the movement to continental unity, as well as remedy the weak-

nesses of the OAU, all of Africa's 53 nation-states joined the new organization. Libyan leader Muammar Gadhafi, who favors the establishment of a "United States of Africa," was one of the leading advocates for increasing the pace of African unity.

The African Union's structure is loosely modeled on that of the European Union. One of its institutions is the Pan-African Parliament, which was inaugurated in March 2004. There are also plans to establish a Court of Justice and three financial institutions—a central bank, monetary fund, and investment bank.

ECONOMIC INTEGRATION

Various other organizations working to forge economic integration among countries in Africa have been established over the years. Currently there are approximately 30 regional trade arrangements, with African countries belonging on average to at least four different trade groups.

Five main economic communities serve as building blocks for an African-wide monetary union (in which nations agree to fix the exchange rates of their currencies and follow a common monetary policy). These organizations are the Arab Monetary Union, the Common Market for Eastern and Southern Africa (COMESA), the Economic Community of Central African States (ECCAS), the Economic Community of West African States (ECOWAS), and the Southern African Development Community (SADC).

In addition, there are three regional monetary unions in Africa: the Common Monetary Area (CMA), which includes Lesotho, Namibia, South Africa, and Swaziland; the Economic and Monetary Community for Central Africa (CAEMC), which contains Cameroon, the Central African Republic, Chad, the Republic of the Congo, Equatorial Guinea, and Gabon; and the West African Economic Union (WAEMU), which comprises Benin, Burkina Faso, Cote d'Ivoire, Guinea–Bissau, Mali, Niger, Senegal, and Togo. The CMA is based on South Africa's rand currency, while countries in the CAEMC and WAEMU use the CFA franc. (CFA stands for Financial Cooperation in Central Africa, and in Western Africa it is the abbreviation for the Financial Community of Africa.)

However, the effectiveness of Africa's regional economic organizations in promoting close economic ties and harmonizing the economic policies of their members has been mixed. Trade among African nations declined during the late 1970s, although it recovered in the 1980s and in the late 1990s reached about 10 percent, where it has remained. In its 2004 report *Assessing Regional Integration in Africa*, the United Nations Economic Commission for Africa noted that regional integration in Africa has produced few concrete results. Some economists consider today's Africa to be the least economically integrated region in the world and least open to internal trade.

There are many reasons for the slow pace of trade among African countries. Most of Africa's economies are agricultural and produce many similar products. As a result, there are fewer commodities to trade among nations. The duplication and overlapping of memberships within the various regional organizations have also hampered their effectiveness, and sometimes led to inconsistent aims in African economic initiatives. Most of the organizations are underfunded and lack the technical capacity to achieve their goals.

Perhaps the most important reason for the lack of progress in regional economic integration is that governments in Africa have lacked the political will and ideological mindset to steer their respective countries in that direction. Despite their rhetoric supporting unity, many African governments remain averse to liberalizing their trade, even with their neighbors, and believe in protectionism—establishing policies that keep out foreign goods and services in order to protect local producers.

IMPACT OF ETHNIC NATIONALISM

Regional economic integration has also been hampered by the rise of ethnic nationalism within certain areas of Africa. Soon after independence, it became clear that many of the newly formed multicultural nations did not have sufficient resources to provide the material development promised to all of their citizens. Often only certain ethnic groups benefited from the construction of roads, water pipelines, electricity infrastructure, hospitals, and schools, while other groups did not. By the late 1960s, these disadvantaged groups had lost faith in the authority and legitimacy of their governments. Disillusioned with their government's attempt to build a multicultural nation, some people became more receptive to the ethnic nationalist ideas being propagated by political leaders who claimed that material progress was best achieved by pursuing ethnic or regional interests.

Today, ethnic nationalism and ethnicity have become important political issues throughout sub-Saharan Africa. Some ethnic groups are striving to break away from African countries and become independent nation-states. This recourse to ethnic or racial nationalism futher hinders the already difficult job individual governments have of creating a multicultural, unified nation and of furthering economic development and integration.

An example of ethnic nationalism in Nigeria is the movement by the Ijaw group, whose members are indigenous to the oil-producing Niger Delta region. Since Nigeria's independence, the Ijaws increasingly have come to view themselves as belonging to a single Ijaw nation, and not as part of the country. The development of Ijaw nationalism is largely a response to the discovery and exploitation of oil on their land. Ethnic nationalism has also been fuelled by feelings of injustice at the environmental damage caused by oil production activities, as well as by the desire of some locals to obtain a share of the oil wealth. Attacks on oil

Ethnic nationalism not only hampers efforts to unite nations, but can also lead to violence and terrorism. Militants with the Movement for the Emancipation of the Niger Delta, shown here, claim to be working for the rights of the Ijaw people of Nigeria. The group's methods include the kidnapping of oil workers and attacks on oil production facilities.

installations and kidnappings of foreign oil workers have threatened to destabilize Nigeria's oil industry.

UNEVEN ECONOMIC DEVELOPMENT

Regional integration in Africa has been hindered by uneven economic development across the continent, which is apparent by the significant differences in national incomes found throughout sub-Saharan Africa. The richest country in the region, Seychelles, has a per capita income of over $7,000, while the poorest nations report less than $300. Among the more prosperous African countries are Mauritius, Botswana, and South Africa.

Countries with weak economies believe they are unlikely to gain much from opening up their borders to their more prosperous neighbors. Because the former fear domination by the latter, they are often reluctant to dismantle border barriers to the free movement of people, goods, and resources. For instance, the launch of the East African Customs Union in January 2005 was delayed partly because Ugandan businessmen feared competition from the more economically dominant Kenya.

On the other hand, countries with large economies are also sometimes hesitant to integrate their economies with smaller, less economically sound neighbors because of the likelihood of monetary losses. Nigeria has been slow to harmonize its tariff system with those of its neighbors in ECOWAS because of concerns that lowering tariffs would lead to an influx of lower-priced Asian imports entering the country via Nigeria's poor neighbors.

Many African governments believe that integration of their nations' economies will promote economic diversification and boost trade. Economic integration would also boost Africa's profile in the global economy, transforming it into a strong united bloc on par with the European Union and the United States.

These African leaders believe that Africa's participation as a unified bloc in globalization would ensure economic stability and bring a higher standard of living to Africa's impoverished nations.

However, the likelihood of a united Africa participating in the global economy in the near future remains doubtful. Unlike economic consolidation in Europe, North America, and South America, regional integration efforts in Africa have done little to date to accelerate growth or increase regional trade. The establishment of enlarged regional markets in Africa has not expanded trade within regions, overcome the constraints of operating in small markets, or prompted investment in larger industrial projects, as was expected. The lack of discernable benefits has discouraged Africa's private sectors from supporting projects to advance regional economic unity. African businesses continue to look inward or focus on transactions with the West and with Asia. With the exception of South Africa, African countries contain very few multinational companies with operations in other African countries.

Nevertheless, African political leaders, policymakers, and intellectuals have in recent decades stressed the importance of seeking African solutions to African problems. This is partly a response to the continent's continued dependency on foreign aid and initiatives of foreign governments and organizations. It also reflects wariness of some leaders about globalization, which many Africans see as the latest manifestation of the domination of nonwhite nations by Western nations.

DEBT IN SUB-SAHARAN AFRICA

Some Africans view international trade as a system that disadvantages, even victimizes, developing countries. And sub-Saharan Africa is said to be the most victimized region, where persistent poverty and underdevelopment exists in almost all of its nations.

Economic crises hit many African countries in the late 1970s, when there was a slump in world commodity prices (the prices that African nations get on the global market for its tradable goods, which include minerals and agricultural products such as oil, diamonds, gold, platinum, exotic woods, cocoa and coffee). As a result many countries turned to the World Bank and International Monetary Fund (IMF) for financial assistance. However, the loans from these institutions were conditional. To obtain them, governments were required to restructure their economies by reducing state control and promoting free market reforms according to the IMF's Structural Adjustment Program (SAP). SAP policies required devaluation of overvalued national currencies, financial liberalization, tax reforms, privatization of inefficient state enterprises, removal of barriers to foreign investment, and trade liberalization.

Faida Mitifu, ambassador of the Democratic Republic of the Congo, and Rosa Whitaker of the African Growth and Opportunity Act (AGOA) action committee discuss investment in Africa with World Bank president Paul Wolfowitz in June 2005. By the early 21st century, many African nations had accumulated huge debts, in part because of conditional loans obtained through the World Bank and International Monetary Fund.

Free market reforms were not popular in Africa. Governments often only partially implemented them and other reforms prescribed by the IMF to help them get out of their financial crises. Even so, many African analysts argue that SAP policies resulted in African nations becoming even more dependent on the West than they had been during colonialism.

While Africa's leaders remain suspicious of the motives of industrialized nations in offering aid, debt relief, and trade concessions, some continue to rest much of their hopes in securing assistance. However, many Africans continue to disapprove of Western values, such as individualism, competition, and materialism, and seek African solutions to matters of development.

AFRICA AS A CAUSE

Outside Africa, particularly in industrialized nations, many people share the view that the region has been the victim of an unfair, and even predatory, global system. They see it as an unfortunate place that the developed world needs to help. Western politicians, institutions, and international aid agencies have in recent years argued that Africa's development is the responsibility not only of Africans but also of the international community, or more specifically, of the rich world.

Africa has long been a cause for people in Western Europe and the United States. However, since the 1990s expressions of concern have become more intense. In 2001 Britain's prime minister, Tony Blair, described Africa as "a scar on the conscience of the world" that the world had a duty to heal. He called for "a partnership for Africa, between the developed and developing world."

Various schemes have been established by Western European and U.S. governments to assist economic development in Africa, including the United Kingdom's Commission for Africa and the United States' Initiative to End Hunger in Africa. In July 2005, at the G8 Gleneagles summit in Scotland, the heads of state of the world's eight leading industrialized countries announced a commitment to double development assistance to poor countries by the end of the decade—from $25 billion in 2004 to $50 billion in 2010, with 25 billion allocated for Africa. They also agreed to write off $40 billion worth of debt owed by 18 of the world's poorest countries, most of which are in Africa.

International charity organizations working to alleviate world poverty have also given particular attention to Africa. It has become common to see international music pop stars and other celebrities calling for increased foreign aid for Africa, as happened in the massive Band Aid and Live8 concerts held in 1985 and 2005, respectively. Africa is the central focus of the Make Poverty History campaign, launched in 2005 by a coalition of charities, religious groups, and trade unions.

However, the role of foreign aid in the development of poor countries can be controversial. Of greater importance, some

At the end of the G8 summit held July 8, 2005, in Gleneagles, Scotland, African leaders stand with the heads of the eight most industrialized nations as British prime minister Tony Blair speaks. At the meeting, G8 leaders agreed to combat poverty in Africa by pledging $25 billion in aid to sub-Saharan Africa.

African leaders point out, is foreign investment, which can lead to economic growth. "If you build a road but don't encourage investment," Jakaya M. Kikwete, the president of Tanzania, said in 2006, "at the end of the day, you come back and you find people as poor as they were when you built the road."

Critics of foreign aid say that the relationship now existing between Africa and the West is similar to the relationship that existed between European imperial powers and their colonies, except that it is no longer bilateral (that is between the colony and its administrative country), but multilateral (between various industrialized nations and Africa). Opponents of foreign aid maintain that Africa has come under virtual international tutelage, with Western-led development agencies such as the World Bank and the International Monetary Fund (IMF) charged with teaching and overseeing the continent's development.

MEETING MILLENNIUM DEVELOPMENT GOALS

While other parts of the developing world are moving forward, many African states are as badly off today as they were in the 1960s. Some nations have even regressed since the early 1980s. In an effort to address problems of Africa and other impoverished regions of the world, the international community of the United Nations established the Millennium Development Goals (MDGs). They call on countries to meet certain objectives by 2015 to help eradicate extreme poverty and defeat diseases such as HIV, AIDS, and malaria. Africa is the only continent that remains behind on most MDGs.

Although economic growth data show that other developing regions, such as China and India, have made significant progress over the past three decades, Africa's slow economy is barely keeping up with the continent's quickly expanding population. During the last two decades, the number of poor in Africa has

In 2000 the United Nations approved the Millennium Development Goals (MDGs), a set of eight objectives aimed at helping lift the world's poorest people out of extreme poverty. At the September 2005 UN General Assembly, shown here, progress on meeting these MDG targets was discussed. Some analysts believe Africa will be the one region that will fail to meet these goals by the 2015 deadline.

doubled from 150 million to 300 million. It now makes up more than 40 percent of the population.

While Asia still has the largest number of people living in extreme poverty in the world, Africa has the largest in proportion to population size. The percentage of Africans living on less than a dollar a day was greater in 2000 than it was in 1990. According to the United Nations Development Program (UNDP), the world's 25 least-developed countries are all in sub-Saharan Africa. Literacy levels in the region have fallen from 50 percent in 1990 to 37 percent in 2000.

Meanwhile, life expectancy in sub-Saharan Africa has fallen drastically since the 1980s. Major decreases in life expectancy are due in part to the AIDS pandemic, which has had the greatest impact in the countries of South Africa, Lesotho, Botswana, and Zimbabwe. These nations and many other sub-Saharan countries have been forced to deal with the long-term economic damage of AIDS (such as the loss of experienced workers and their income). An estimated 25 million have been infected by HIV/AIDS, and preventing the spread of the deadly virus to the remaining 700 million who have not been infected remains a priority.

BUILDING POLITICAL AND ECONOMIC INSTITUTIONS

Although regional averages for most social and economic indicators clearly show Africa lagging well behind other parts of the world, these figures sometimes give a distorted picture of the complex reality in the continent. Africa includes a wide range of economies—some are grossly underperforming while others are doing reasonably well. For instance, since the mid-1990s 16 countries in sub-Saharan Africa have demonstrated annual gross

Young children who have lost one or both parents to AIDS attend a day program in South Africa. UNICEF estimates that by 2010 the deadly disease could orphan as many as 18 million children in sub-Saharan Africa.

domestic product growth rates in excess of 4.5 percent. In several of these countries, including Ghana, Uganda, Mozambique, Tanzania, and Senegal, the higher growth rates has been accompanied by diversification of their economies.

The common image of Africa as a place ruled by corrupt governments that have mismanaged their economies and continue to do so can also be misleading, and it has deterred foreign investment. Although Africa has had more than its fair share of weak, incompetent, and predatory states, some countries have made significant advancements in building political and economic institutions to support development and reduce poverty. Many states have taken measures to strengthen property rights, overhaul judicial systems, and generally improve economic management.

Countries such as Botswana and Mauritius have demonstrated strong economic growth—largely because of their effective political and economic institutions, which have promoted good governance. Several other sub-Saharan Africa nations with similarly strong foundations, such as Mozambique, Uganda, Mali, Senegal, and Ghana, show promise of becoming strong economic performers as well.

Some IMF researchers believe that although institutions are generally weak in Africa, in parts of the region they are strong enough to support increased economic growth. Over the past decade, countries that have seen increased economic growth have also seen reductions in poverty rates. In contrast, countries with low economic growth rates have seen increases in poverty rates.

INVESTING IN AFRICA

While sub-Saharan African countries face enormous problems of severe poverty and underdevelopment, the tendency to equate Africa with perennial poverty and underdevelopment is not only misinformed but also potentially harmful to the region. Some politicians and antipoverty activists, inside and outside Africa, perpetuate this image because it supports the case for increasing foreign aid to the continent. Images of starving children in war-scarred Sierra Leone are likely to stir more sympathy from donors in industrialized nations than pictures of prospering entrepreneurs in Senegal.

However, lumping together all Africans in one basket of misery can be harmful to those African nations that are trying to develop economically through foreign investment. Since the mid-1980s foreign investment flows to developing countries have tended to concentrate on parts of the world considered to be economically dynamic, such as East Asia, and especially China, which is seen as strong and self-reliant.

In contrast, investors have been shy of Africa, even though some states in the region have investment climates that are as good as those found in Asia. Of total investments made in developing countries, Africa's share fell from an average of 17.4 percent in the 1970s to just 5.1 percent in the 1990s. While its share has risen in recent years, it was still less than 9 percent in 2003 (as compared with a peak of 28 percent in 1976).

Africa now accounts for just 2 to 3 percent of global foreign direct investment (FDI) flow, a decrease from a peak of 6 percent in the mid-1970s. The bulk of FDI in Africa is concentrated in about a dozen countries and mainly in areas such as mineral extraction. The main investors are countries with historic links with the continent. Between 1980 and 2000 just three countries—France and the United Kingdom (the two former colonial powers) and the United States—accounted for close to 70 percent of total FDI flow to the continent.

Another reason for the low level of foreign investment in Africa, besides the continent's poor image, is that the vast majority of African countries have very small markets. More than half of the countries in Africa have populations of 10 million or less.

Investors seeking to expand their market share prefer places with large pools of skilled labor, as well as good infrastructure. As a result, they have turned to locations in Asia or Latin America, which have greater populations and clusters of industries.

ISOLATIONISM, REGIONALISM, OR GLOBALIZATION

As African leaders seek to improve the lives of the people in their countries, they have several options. They can choose the path of isolationism, or economic nationalism, and work to protect only the interests of businesses within their individual nation. An alternative path would be for them to reach beyond national boundaries to build the regional links to realize the goals of pan-Africanism. Or heads of state can reach out even further, and embrace globalization.

Although advocates of regionalism claim that regional integration is a step towards globalization, the two are arguably quite distinct. Often countries set up regional economic blocs to strengthen ties among themselves and at the same time keep out or discriminate against those who do not belong to the group. This policy runs counter to globalization, which requires the removal of all barriers to the free flow of people, trade, and resources.

In debates over the merits of globalization, its supporters contend that much of the world's prosperity and improved living standards in recent decades derive from the expansion of global trade, investment, migration, information, and technology. Globalization advocates say that these developments have benefited not only rich nations but also poor ones, including those in Africa. Increased foreign investment flows have created tremendous opportunities in poor countries. Studies show that foreign firms bring management capabilities, invest heavily in infrastructure and in the training of workers, and enable host countries to reach large markets. Globalization frees people from the limitations of their immediate environment and opens up a vast new world of possibilities and opportunities, culturally and economically.

Opponents to globalization claim that it exposes poor nations to unfair foreign competition that leads to the ruin of their newly formed industries. In addition, they say, globalization locks developing economies into primary product dependency and exacerbates inequality within and between nations.

Some Africans oppose globalization because protectionist policies help their own personal interests. This is particularly true in regions with high-value natural resources such as oil. The

Ugandan farmers demonstrate against globalization policies in August 2002 in Johannesburg, South Africa. Because many developing countries have agricultural economies, they are adversely affected when the international prices of coffee, cotton, and other cash crops decline. Anti-globalization activists complain that world trade–governing bodies such as the WTO have allowed powerful corporations and rich nations to create trade policies that hurt the economies of developing countries.

extremely high profit made from the exploitation of these resources, referred to by economists as "rent," has led to corruption as leaders and politicians seek to benefit from windfall revenues. These rent-seeking local elites oppose any reforms that undermine their financial interests.

Hostility to global integration may also stem from the fear of some members of the African elites that globalization will further weaken their power. During the past 125 years or so, most of the major political, economic, and cultural changes that have taken place in Africa as elsewhere in the developing world, from the naming of nations to the laws that govern them, have been determined or influenced by people from Western Europe and the United States. Nationalism is a means by which the unconfident elites hope to regain control and authority in their societies. By keeping out foreign competition, protectionism enables local elites to maintain their privileged positions within their societies.

Perhaps the best way for African leaders to approach the question of which path their peoples should tread—isolation, regionalism, or globalization—is to consider the matter from the perspective that the primary purpose of government should be to defend the rights of its citizens.

In June 2006, at the World Economic Forum on Africa, held in Cape Town, South African president Thabo Mbeki discussed the importance of democratic governments to Africa's future: "For many of our countries, the big challenge is developing multicultural, multiethnic, multifaith, multilingual societies which don't cohere naturally," Mbeki said.

> The best way to manage societies like these is indeed to make them as democratic as possible. You can't hold societies like this together by force or deceit or deals among the elites. In the end, you've got to make sure the population participates in all of these processes.

Some people believe that the increase in multiparty democratic elections and the peaceful transitions of power that have

At the June 2006 World Economic Forum on Africa, which met in Cape Town, South Africa, attendees reviewed reports of Africa's strongest economic growth in three decades—5.5 percent in 2005.

occurred in African countries since the 1990s are a sign that Africa is building the political institutions it needs to support development. The path to good governance was furthered for African women and democracy in 2005 with the election in Liberia of Ellen Johnson-Sirleaf, who became Africa's first elected female leader.

CHRONOLOGY

1518	First direct shipment of slaves from Africa to the West Indies.
1652	Dutch colony is founded in the Cape of Good Hope.
1807	Britain abolishes slave trade, although ownership continues.
1822	Liberia is established as a colony for freed slaves.
1834	Britain outlaws ownership of slaves.
1884–85	Berlin Conference partitions Africa among European powers.
1888	Slavery is abolished in Brazil, bringing an end to legally sanctioned slavery in the western hemisphere.
1900	First Pan-African conference held in London to protest theft of lands in colonies and racial discrimination.
1910	Union of South Africa formed.
1935	Italy invades Abyssinia (Ethiopia), provoking outcry from African nationalists.
1945	The fifth Pan-African Congress is held in Manchester, England.
1948	First apartheid legislation is passed in South Africa.
1952	Mau Mau rebellion against British colonial rule erupts in Kenya.

CHRONOLOGY

1954	Gamal Abdel Nasser takes power in Egypt.
1956	Egyptian leader Gamal Abdel Nasser nationalizes the Suez Canal, which leads to the invasion of Egypt by Britain, France, and Israel.
1957	Ghana becomes the first independent sub-Saharan African nation.
1960	Nigeria, Côte d' Ivoire, Chad, Gabon, Mali, Senegal and many other African colonies become independent; nationalist leader Patrice Lumumba becomes first prime minister of newly independent Congo.
1961	Patrice Lumumba is assassinated; South Africa is declared a republic and leaves the British Commonwealth.
1962	Algeria wins independence from France.
1963	Kenya declares independence from British; the Organization of African Unity is formed.
1964	Nelson Mandela and other African National Congress leaders are sentenced to life imprisonment.
1965	White-minority government in Rhodesia declares independence from British Commonwealth.
1966	Nigeria's civilian government falls in the country's first military coup.
1967–70	Nigerian civil war with secessionist Biafra in which almost one million people die of starvation.
1971	Idi Amin rises to power in a coup in Uganda.

1972	The Addis Ababa Agreement ends the first Sudanese Civil War.
1979	Tanzania invades Uganda, precipitating the downfall of dictator Amin.
1980	Black majority rule established in Zimbabwe (formerly Rhodesia) after nationalist Robert Mugabe wins election.
1994	Anti-apartheid activist Nelson Mandela elected president in South Africa; approximately 800,000 ethnic Tutsis and moderate Hutus massacred by Hutu extremists in Rwanda.
1997	Congo's notoriously corrupt president, Mobutu Sese Seko, is overthrown by rebel forces led by Laurent Kabila.
1998	Congo becomes battleground of international conflict with rebels backed by Rwanda and Uganda fighting Kabila while Zimbabwe, Namibia, and Angola support him.
2001	The New Partnership for Africa's Development (NEPAD) is adopted by the OAU as the blueprint for tackling underdevelopment in the continent, with the aid of developed nations.
2002	African Union (AU) is established as successor organization of the OAU to promote unity among Africa's 53 states.
2005	Ellen Johnson-Sirleaf is sworn in as president of Liberia, becoming continent's first elected female leader.

GLOSSARY

AFRICAN DIASPORA—people from Africa or whose ancestors are from Africa and who are living outside their homeland.

CAPITALISM—an economic system based on private ownership and characterized by competition and the profit motive.

CIVILIZATION—a society in an advanced state of social development.

COLONIALISM—the extension of a nation's sovereignty over territory and people outside its own boundaries.

CULTURE—the ideas, customs, values, and art that a group of people share.

DECOLONIZATION—the process by which a colony gains independence from a colonial power.

ETHNOCENTRISM—the belief that one's own group or culture is superior to all other groups or cultures.

GROSS DOMESTIC PRODUCT (GDP)—the total value of goods and services produced in a nation.

IDEOLOGY—set of beliefs that explain or justify an organization's decisions and behavior.

IMPERIALISM—the practice of one country extending its control over the territory, political system, or economic life of another country.

GLOSSARY

INDIGENOUS—originating in a place.

NATIONALISM—the belief that the culture and interests of one's nation are superior to those of any other nation.

NEW WORLD—collective name for North and South America and adjacent islands.

SOCIALISM—an economic or political system based on collective and governmental ownership.

SUPRANATIONAL—transcending established national boundaries or spheres of interest.

TRADITIONAL—conforming to established practice or standards.

TUTELAGE—influence or authority over a foreign territory.

WESTERN—describing nations and cultures of Western Europe and North America.

FURTHER READING

Davidson, Basil. *Discovering Africa's Past.* London: Longman Group, 1978.

French, Howard W. *A Continent for the Taking: The Tragedy and Hope of Africa.* New York: Vintage Books, 2005.

Guest, Robert. *The Shackled Continent: Africa's Past, Present and Future.* London: Macmillan, 2004.

Lamb, David. *The Africans: Encounters from the Sudan to the Cape.* London: Methuen, 1985.

McEvedy, Colin. *The Penguin Atlas of African History.* London: Penguin Books, 1995.

Meredith, Martin. *The Fate of Africa: From the Hopes of Freedom to the Heart of Despair.* New York: PublicAffairs, 2005.

Sagay, J. O., and D. A. Wilson. *Africa: A Modern History (1800–1975)*, London: Evans Brothers, 1978.

INTERNET RESOURCES

HTTP://WWW.AFRICA-UNION.ORG

The website of the African Union.

HTTP://WWW.UN.ORG/ECOSOCDEV/GENINFO/AFREC/

Africa Renewal Online Magazine published by the United Nations Department of Public Information.

HTTP://WWW.BBC.CO.UK/WORLDSERVICE/AFRICA/FEATURES/STORYOFAFRICA/INDEX.SHTML

BBC website tells the history of Africa from an African perspective.

HTTP://WWW.LOC.GOV/EXHIBITS/AFRICAN/AFAM001.HTML

A Library of Congress Resource Guide for the Study of Black History & Culture.

HTTP://WWW-SUL.STANFORD.EDU/DEPTS/SSRG/AFRICA/HISTORY.HTML

Comprehensive website on Africa, South of the Sahara.

HTTP://WWW.FORDHAM.EDU/HALSALL/AFRICA/AFRICASBOOK.HTML

Internet African History Sourcebooks, edited by Paul Halsall, History Department, Fordham University, New York.

HTTP://WWW.ALLAFRICA.COM

A comprehensive internet portal for news and features on African countries.

Publisher's Note: The websites listed on this page were active at the time of publication. The publisher is not responsible for websites that have changed their address or discontinued operation since the date of publication. The publisher will review and update the websites each time the book is reprinted.

INDEX

Numbers in ***bold italic*** refer to captions.

INDEX

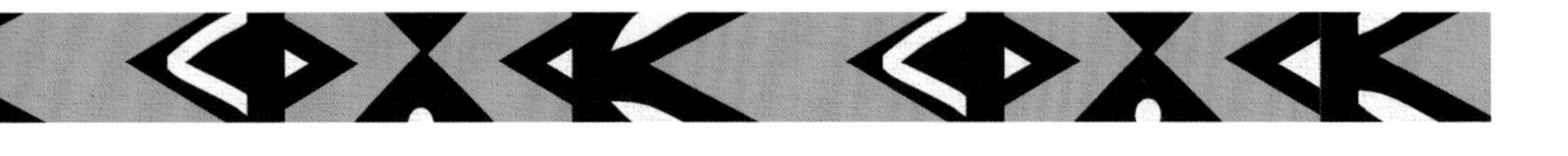

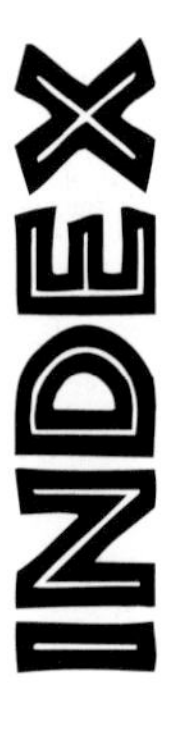
INDEX

INDEX

INDEX

PICTURE CREDITS

Page
2: Jim Watson/AFP/Getty Images
9: © OTTN Publishing
12: Corbis Images
16: Library of Congress
19: Library of Congress
21: Werner Forman/Corbis
23: Library of Congress
24: Bowers Museum of Cultural Art/Corbis
26: Photographs Copyright © 2003 IMS Communications Ltd., www.picture-gallery.com
29: Robert Caputo/Aurora/Getty Images
33: Corbis
34: Jan Rosvoral
38: Bojan Brecelj/Corbis
41: Bettmann/Corbis
44: © OTTN Publishing
47: Hulton Archive/Getty Images
49: Mansell/Time & Life Pictures/Getty Images
51: Library of Congress
53: Bettmann/Corbis
54: Hulton Archive/Getty Images
57: Fox Photos/Getty Images
61: Library of Congress
63: Library of Congress
65: Library of Congress
68: C.M. Battey/Getty Images
69: MPI/Getty Images
73: John Deakin/Picture Post/Hulton Archive/Getty Images
75: Library of Congress
77: Central Press/Getty Images
78: AFP/AFP/Getty Images
81: AFP/Getty Images
84: Keystone/Getty Images
86: Central Press/Getty Images
89: Scott Peterson/Liaison/Getty Images
91: Eric Feferberg/AFP/Getty Images
93: Walter Dhladhla/AFP/Getty Images
94: Gianluigi Guercia/AFP/Getty Images
97: Alexander Joe/AFP/Getty Images
100: Dave Clark/AFP/Getty Images
103: Joe Raedle/Getty Images
105: Michael Kappeler/AFP/Getty Images
107: Michael Nagle/Getty Images
108: Alexander Joe/AFP/Getty Images
112: Yoav Lemmer/AFP/Getty Images
114: Gianluigi Guercia/AFP/Getty Images

Front cover: Top Photos (left to right): Alexander Joe/AFP/Getty Images; Scott Peterson/Liaison/Getty Images; Desirey Minkoh/AFP/Getty Images

Back cover: Collage of images created by OTTN Publishing with images provided by US AID

CONTRIBUTORS

PROFESSOR ROBERT I. ROTBERG is Director of the Program on Intrastate Conflict and Conflict Resolution at the Kennedy School, Harvard University, and President of the World Peace Foundation. He is the author of a number of books and articles on Africa, including *A Political History of Tropical Africa* and *Ending Autocracy, Enabling Democracy: The Tribulations of Southern Africa.*

TUNDE OBADINA, B.S., M.A., is a journalist and economist. He has worked for a number of organizations, including the British Broadcasting Corporation (BBC) and Reuters News agency. He is currently the director of Africa Business Information Service and is an external author for the Economist Intelligence Unit.